Alcohol
and
Alcoholism

MEMBERSHIP OF THE SPECIAL COMMITTEE
ON ALCOHOLISM

Dr T. H. Bewley,
Dean, Royal College of Psychiatrists. Consultant Psychiatrist, St Thomas's and Tooting Bec Hospitals. Consultant Adviser on Dependence, Department of Health and Social Security.

Dr P. H. Connell,
Director, Drug Dependency Clinical Research and Treatment Unit, the Bethlem Royal and Maudsley Hospital.

Dr G. Edwards (Chairman),
Honorary Director, Addiction Research Unit, Institute of Psychiatry, London.

Dr M. M. Glatt,
Honorary Consultant Physician, Department of Psychological Medicine, University College Hospital. Medical Director, Galsworthy House, Kingston-on-Thames. Formerly Consultant-in-Charge, Regional Alcoholism and Drug Dependence Unit, St Bernard's Hospital.

Dr H. B. Milne,
Consultant-in-Charge, Forensic Psychiatric Unit, Waddiloves Hospital, Bradford.

Dr R. M. Murray,
Senior Lecturer, Institute of Psychiatry, London.

Dr A. N. Oppenheim,
Reader in Social Psychology, London School of Economics.

Professor H. J. Walton,
Professor of Psychiatry, University of Edinburgh. Consultant in Psychiatry, Royal Edinburgh Hospital. Director of the Department of Psychiatry, Western General Hospital, Edinburgh.

Observer
Dr A. Sippert,
Medical Officer with special interest in addiction, Department of Health and Social Security, London.

Secretary
Mrs Gail Lloyd

Alcohol and Alcoholism

*The Report of a Special Committee of
the Royal College of Psychiatrists*

Foreword by
SIR MARTIN ROTH

THE FREE PRESS
A Division of Macmillan Publishing Co., Inc.
NEW YORK

The Free Press
A Division of Macmillan Publishing Co., Inc.
866 Third Avenue, New York, N.Y. 10022

Collier Macmillan Canada, Ltd.

First American Edition 1979

Library of Congress Catalog Card Number: 79-20712

Printed in the United States of America

printing number

1 2 3 4 5 6 7 8 9 10

Library of Congress Cataloging in Publication Data

Royal College of Psychiatrists.
    Alcohol & alcoholism.

    Bibliography: p.
    Includes index.
    1. Alcoholism--Great Britain--Congresses.
2. Alcoholics--Great Britain--Psychology--Congresses.
I. Title.
HV5444.R69 1979   616.8'61   79-20712
ISBN 0-02-927510-5

Contents

Foreword

Serious alcohol dependence is the most striking example of that characteristically modern group of maladies which originates from behaviour that is ostensibly controlled by the free choice of individual sufferers. Each member of the community is theoretically at liberty to decide for himself whether he takes alcohol in moderation or excess, whether or not he smokes cigarettes, or sniffs cocaine, eats in a frugal or gluttonous manner, drives as fast as he can or never at a speed above 55 miles per hour. But as such disorders appear at first sight to have more kinship with self-indulgence than disease they have been regarded in the past as falling more within the realm of interest of moralists and theologians and the law than medicine, public health, and government. Although the ill effects of drunkenness and gluttony have been widely recognized for many centuries it is only within recent decades that this whole group of phenomena has come to be increasingly recognized as being of central importance for clinical and preventive medicine.

Each presents obdurate problems of its own and in none has a satisfactory solution been found. Once a substance or a form of conduct that relieves unpleasant emotions or promotes gratifying ones has become widely prevalent, education, exhortation, and legislation are liable to be resented as a presumptious interference with the individual's freedom to live his life as he chooses.

The subject also bristles with paradoxes that impede the development and implementation of rational and coherent policies. The chronic alcoholic undermines his health, destroys his talent and sensibility, and is liable to die prematurely. But in countries in which the production of wine is a major industry there are strong economic reasons for keeping alive the myth that the daily consumption of substantial quantities of alcohol is indispensable for health and strength. It is true that if by some miracle the majority of individuals in a community could be induced to abandon the alcoholic habit overnight the immediate effect would be a steep increase in unemployment and in some cases economic ruin. Governments are therefore prone to invoke the freedom of the individual and the danger of a criminally organized black market to justify their unwillingness to intervene.

A candid exposition of the economic facts and arguments that inform such attitudes would be more healthy and constructive than a smokescreen of discreet silence. It would open the way for scientists to adduce and disseminate the factual evidence that, when the vast hidden cost of the social miseries that stem from alcoholism are taken into account, legislative action to reduce consumption of alcohol could be taken with economic impunity. And there are sound reasons for anticipating that substantial improvements in the health of the nation would be likely to follow.

Dr Griffith Edwards and his Committee have managed to compress into a small volume a remarkably comprehensive account of the epidemiology, social background, clinical features, and management of alcoholic dependence. As the information that becomes available, for different communities, about the alcohol consumption of individual members is inevitably incomplete, the ills to which it contributes and the demands it causes upon health and welfare services have never been fully estimated. The known facts as summarized in this Report tell a woeful tale. Many reasonably informed people are familiar with delirium tremens and liver disease as complications of alcoholism. The part it plays in causation of diseases of the pancreas, cancer of the oesophagus and stomach, tuberculosis, anaemia, vitamin deficiency, and some grave forms of heart disease are less well known.

Even greater ignorance prevails regarding the wide range of mental disorders associated with chronic alcoholic dependence. Delirium tremens may be familiar but the paranoid psychoses that arise in the course of alcoholism including the states of morbid jealousy that place wives at grave risk of injury and death are far less well known. Alcoholism appears to function as a catalyst so that it accentuates and brings to light dispositions in mental suffering that might otherwise have remained dormant. It may be associated with states of profound depression and contributes substantially to the causation both of attempted and consummated suicide. There are also chronic hallucinatory states and other disorders of the mind that some psychiatrists would regard as having close kinship with the schizophrenic family of disorders.

The alcoholic individual is more than his own executioner. Here the disorder differs from some of the other conditions mentioned in the first paragraph. The suffering is not confined to the individual. It engulfs those in his family circle and social environment. Some handicaps are transmitted to the next generation and we know that this does not occur as a result of heredity alone. The spouse suffers emotional and material deprivation and the personalities of the children may be warped in their formative years. Wives who are battered and children who are abused often have parents in whom alcoholic dependence figures among other personality difficulties. A great deal of the crime that complicates the disorder is of a petty kind but not all of it. The drift down the social scale, unemployment, and the association with traffic accidents have all been well documented.

The authors have laid emphasis on one important fact for which an increasing body of evidence has accumulated in recent years. This is that consumption per head of the population and the damage to health caused by alcohol are closely associated, though in ways that are poorly understood. In the light of this the increase of annual *per capita* consumption of alcohol in the United Kingdom in the period between 1950 and 1976 from 5·2 litres to 9·7 litres gives cause for grave concern. Incomplete evidence in no way justifies inaction in the face of an epidemic of this dimension. This report is in the best traditions of the public health movement in this country which has in the past so often anticipated by its actions the stringent scientific testimony that later provided the rationale for them.

The Committee appointed by the Royal College of Psychiatrists makes it clear that it is not in a position to cite causal agents or remedies of proven value. It is Sherrington who has provided the most eloquent justification for the course of action embodied in its Report: 'Science nobly can wait for an answer; common-sense pressed for time must act from acceptance.'

The Committee has summarized the available evidence clearly and cogently and its Report is comprehensible to health authorities, medical practitioners, and the general public alike. No matter how great their expertise and experience there will be few who will read it without profit. Governments and communities are invited to '. . . look beyond the statistics to the personal realities of suffering from a wasted life and family miseries'. Realistic goals are set for a programme of prevention in which a commitment by government to education of the public has an important part to play. The specific recommendations about the content of programmes of education deserve the closest attention of those in a position to carry them into effect. The upper limit of daily drinking suggested here is likely to be widely quoted and it is to be hoped that the heed paid to it will be commensurate. There is of course an implicit assumption that the amount consumed by the average member of the community will have to be substantially below such an 'upper limit' if progress is to be made in the foreseeable future.

It is also implicit in the arguments advanced that intervention by departments of health and governments can achieve little unless there is a parallel change in personal attitudes. The Report is timely for there are signs of a burgeoning of interest, among ordinary people, in what is known about the springs of individual behaviour and the factors that cause it to diverge into self-destructive channels. This quest springs in part from a deepening dissatisfaction with the quality of life within the large cities of affluent societies. And alcoholism is shown by this Report to be prominent among the influences that engender and perpetuate the many forms of human deprivation that characterize such communities.

In short this Report by Dr Griffith Edwards and his Committee under the aegis of the Royal College of Psychiatrists satisfies a variety of previously unmet needs and therefore fills a large gap in the available literature of alcohol dependence. It deserves to be widely read. And implementation of its main recommendations would probably mark a turning point in the attack on the multitude of ills that originate in alcoholism.

Sir Martin Roth, M.D., F.R.C.P., F.R.C.Psych., Sc.D.
Professor of Psychiatry, University of Cambridge.
Past President, Royal College of Psychiatrists.

Acknowledgements

We warmly acknowledge our debt of gratitude to Mrs Gail Lloyd who acted as Secretary to the College's Special Committee on Alcoholism. We are very grateful to Dr David Hirst for preparing the index. Mrs Julia Polglaze gave unfailingly patient help in preparing successive drafts of this Report.

The authors and publishers are grateful to the various individuals and publishers who have given permission for material to be reproduced.

Table 6 on page 95 is reproduced from *Alcohol Control Policies in Public Health Perspective* (1975) by K. Bruun *et al*. with the permission of the Finnish Foundation for Alcohol Studies.

Figure 2 on page 97 is reproduced from *Health Bulletin* 32 (1) with the permission of the Controller of Her Majesty's Stationery Office, by permission of Drs Semple and Yarrow.

I

Why this Report
has been written

Introduction

Alcohol is a substance which is used wisely and well by the majority of people who drink, and who derive nothing but pleasure and benefit from its use. Alcohol is also a drug which can miserably wreck or destroy life, and which exacts these costs on a devastating scale.

Given the equal truth of these two statements it is not surprising that a balanced perspective on alcohol has so far eluded society's grasp. The obvious reaction is to fly to extremes. Some people may be resentful, or resistant, when confronted with forceful evidence about the human costs of a substance which gives them pleasure, and the use of which is deeply embedded in pleasant custom. The tendency will be to dismiss the casualties as few in number, and to stigmatize them as undeserving – they are said to be the over-indulgent fringe who can give any pleasure a bad name, and their wounds are self-inflicted. In this way people who have been harmed by drink are mentally disposed of as undesirables. Alternatively the problem can be tidied away with an appearance of greater generosity by regarding excessive drinkers as sick rather than bad: their drinking is symptomatic of underlying illness, and they must be handed over to the medical profession for treatment. With this sad minority thus kindly dealt with, the rest of us may, with good conscience, go unworried on our drinking way. Whether the excessive drinker is labelled as bad or ill, society all too readily neutralizes its own anxieties.

The contrary reaction, and certainly not the one that wins the majority vote, is to exaggerate the dangers of alcohol and see its use as an unmitigated evil. Drinking itself becomes the devil to be cast out of individual and society alike.

Neither of these extreme reactions serves society well. Their harm lies not only in misleading the individual about his own or his neighbour's drinking, but also in misinforming large-scale national policies. The extreme results can then be either the excesses of Gin Lane, or the excesses of Prohibition.

The fundamental purpose of this Report is to develop a perspective on alcohol and alcoholism which avoids either extreme; a perspective which is based on the most recent evidence but which admits gaps in information where these exist; and which may then accurately serve the needs of the individual, the professional, and the designer of public policies, in a society where alcohol is likely to remain a favoured recreational drug.

Why a report now?

The reasons for believing that it is timely for this Report to be written are several.

Time to respond to a large and threatening problem

A major reason for the timing of this Report is the mass of data which now demonstrate the seriousness of the drinking problems that society is facing. The Report deals not with a minor and peripheral social ill (of a sort worthy of attention only when there is a little reforming energy to spare), but with an endemic disorder of frightening magnitude.

Indeed, the question as to 'the sum of damage' demands an

outline answer immediately, although a full account must be delayed until later. The plain fact is that problems of alcohol abuse constitute an appalling insult to the nation's health, a cause of untold personal and family misery, and a cost to the country of many millions of pounds each year. Such a statement might be thought to call into question the objectivity of this Report, but there is ample factual evidence to support this statement, and to show that it is in no way an exaggeration. We shall give a brief synopsis in the next few paragraphs of some information about damage due to alcohol which will be treated at greater length in Chapter 5.

At a conservative estimate there are at least 300,000 people in this country with drinking problems of such severity as to merit the conventional label of 'alcoholism', and this may well be a gross underestimate. Each of these people is probably affecting the health, happiness, or safety of several family members, friends, and workmates. People with serious drinking problems have an expectation of dying which is between two and three times greater than that of members of the general population of the same age and sex. A recent study in a general hospital in Scotland showed that 25 per cent of acute male admissions to a medical ward were directly or indirectly due to alcohol. Annual National Health Service admissions to psychiatric hospitals for treatment of alcoholism have increased twenty-five-fold over the past twenty years and are now 13,500 per year in England and Wales: the cost of this hospital care alone must now be upwards of £4,000,000 per annum.

That figure is puny by comparison with the non-medical cost of excessive drinking: the Blennerhassett Committee on drunk driving recently estimated that the annual costs of road traffic accidents due to drinking must be about £100,000,000 each year, and drunk driving has been steeply on the increase. Over 100,000 drunkenness arrests are now taken annually through the courts, a figure higher than at any time since before World War II. Drink is implicated in the offences of about 60 per cent of the petty recidivists who contribute so largely to the prison population; without the problems of excessive drinking, the courts would suddenly be underemployed and the prisons remarkably uncrowded. The costs of alcoholism to industry, and the costs in terms of welfare and sickness benefits, must be enormous.

As for the impact on the family, the husband's excessive drinking seems to be implicated in not less than 50 per cent of the cases of wife-battering. The impact of drinking on the psychological development of the children of alcoholics is a painful reality. It is becoming evident that the mother's excessive drinking can damage the unborn child.

The evidence is not only that a problem of great size exists, but one which in nearly every aspect is on an upward climb. There is a rise in such available indices of alcohol misuse as deaths from cirrhosis, hospital admissions for alcoholism, drunkenness arrests, and drunk driving arrests. Underlying these separate changes there is the basic fact that the nation is drinking much more: from 1950 to 1976 the alcohol consumption per head of the adult population increased by 87 per cent. Although each index, taken individually, may be a somewhat uncertain pointer (there can be distortions introduced by such factors as change in diagnostic awareness or in police practice), taken all together the evidence that the problem has grown steadily greater over the years is entirely convincing.

In addition to the general rise in the country's experience of alcohol-related problems, there is much to suggest that within the total population certain groups are now more heavily affected than before. For instance, some teachers report that alcohol rather than drugs is becoming the school-age problem, and they have to deal with children who have been drinking in the lunch-hour. The official figures show a rise in teenage drunkenness – from 1,852 convictions of people aged under eighteen in 1964, to 4,805 in 1976. Doctors report that they are increasingly seeing cirrhosis in a younger age group. There is also much evidence that drinking problems among women are on the increase, and one of the prices to be paid for a more equal place for women in society may be their more equal rate of alcoholism.

The recent increase in alcohol-related problems should not necessarily be taken as proof positive that alcoholism rates are immediately going to surge further out of control. It is possible that over the next few years, and with a standstill or actual fall in

4

real wages and less money to spend on drink, there could be some temporary diminution in drinking problems, so that efforts to win the nation's concern by incautious scare-mongering may lose rather than capture public attention.

The position adopted here is that the threat posed by all these ominous pointers should neither be discounted nor exaggerated, but the information available should remind us that there is no guarantee of immunity from further and explosive increases in these problems. France has for many years had a deathrate from cirrhosis about ten times that in Britain; over the next fifty years, and with all the benefits of Europeanism, we cannot rule out the possibility that drinking and drinking problems will reach uniform and high levels throughout Europe. Many old socio-cultural, legal, and economic barriers may by then have been brought down, and with that overthrow may also go the barriers that have for centuries determined the individuality of different national experiences with drinking. If unchecked by any insistence on health considerations, economic interests might well promote a new level of pan-European problem drinking, a level located much more towards the higher than the lower end of the present spectrum of experiences in separate countries.

In summary, the facts substantiate the conclusion that the problem which we already have is sufficiently serious to constitute an immediate cause for concern. If the casualty rates were to dip to the lowest level recorded in this century, they would still be worrying. If, on the other hand, emancipated adolescents were to drink more like adults, more-liberated women drink more like men, and Britons who have become good Europeans drink more like Frenchmen, then there are threats which are potentially appalling.

Catching a tide of awareness

Over the last couple of decades there has been improvement in this country's awareness about its drinking problems. The nature of some of these developments is charted in Chapter 2. But the very fact of this new activity sets problems. There is the danger of energies being misspent, and of policies being firmly adopted

5

and implemented without sufficient thought being given to the options. One of the reasons for the appearance of this Report, therefore, is that we are at a critical period for the planning of this country's response to drinking problems. If the opportunity is not now seized, options will be closed and a moment for beneficial action will have been lost.

Time to identify the confusions

When few people in the country were particularly concerned about alcoholism, a deceptive clarity of views could be assumed to exist – each side could hold its extreme and straightforward position unchallenged. But varieties of confusion have come about, or have come into sharper focus, as a by-product of the greater interest now taken in drinking problems. It is timely to attempt to identify these confusions (even if they cannot all be resolved), rather than only half-recognizing them when they can persist as pitfalls in planning and social action (see pp. 21–5).

Time to capitalize on new knowledge

There would not be much point in writing a Report if nothing more could be done than itemize the problems and list the confusions. On the contrary, and very fortunately, it should be eminently possible to tackle some of these difficulties in ways not possible before, armed with insights which came from new knowledge on alcohol and alcoholism gained in recent years. This knowledge bears on such questions as the nature of alcohol dependence, why people drink or drink excessively, and the social and cultural influences on rates of alcoholism. But also to be noted is a serious and widening gap between what is known and the use that is being made of the information now readily to hand. Policies on treatment and prevention seem all too often to be based on repetitive application of outdated thinking, rather than on an effort to put research findings to practical use. The time has come to examine the ways in which new knowledge can lead to a restructuring of the nation's response.

The meaning of terms

The word *alcoholism* is in common use, but at the same time there is general uncertainty about its meaning. Where is the dividing line between heavy drinking and this 'illness'? Is it a matter of quantity drunk or damage sustained, or addiction, or of what else besides? This confusion is not limited to the layman, for final clarification has eluded the many experts and expert committees that have grappled with the terms to be used about drinking problems.

For our present purposes, we do not need a greatly detailed theoretical analysis of these problems of definition. A set of ideas and definitions is essential, however, to serve the practical needs of communication, so that when two people talk about matters dealt with in this Report they will be talking about roughly the same things. In the ordinary world a lot of communication constantly centres on abnormal drinking: a wife debating with her husband whether he is or is not an alcoholic, the doctor trying to establish a diagnosis and communicate with his patient, the expression by a psychiatrist or social worker of a professional opinion and the court's attempt to understand exactly what is implied by the technically worded statement, and the facts and arguments being presented to the public on alcohol and health. Because people of many different backgrounds have to find words for communicating with each other, the critical need is for a set of clear definitions which are understood by different professions, and by the world in general.

With this purpose in mind, a brief exposition of the ideas and definitions used in this Report will be given below. These ideas will be taken further in each of the following chapters; here, only an outline will be given. Our presentation will borrow freely from a recent World Health Organization publication (*Alcohol-Related Disabilities* 1977) which tried to meet the challenge of designing a framework of ideas which would not only serve the needs of communication between different people in the same country, but which could also aid communication between different countries.

7

The alcohol dependence syndrome

Alcohol is, in familiar terms, 'a drug of addiction'. The word 'addiction' has, in recent years, rather fallen out of favour because it had become too coloured with the stereotype of narcotic addiction. In this Report the more ungainly phrase *alcohol dependence syndrome* will be used at times to describe the condition which arises when the individual has contracted a dependence on this particular drug. To have less recourse to this ponderous phrase, the Report will usually in context refer simply to 'the syndrome' or 'dependence'. The nature of this condition, and the potentially very serious personal and social implications which will result from this disorder, are dealt with in Chapter 4. It is vital that there should be more general and much fuller understanding about the capacity possessed by society's favoured recreational drug to induce severe dependence.

Alcohol-related disabilities

Although the reality of the alcohol dependence syndrome needs to be brought very much to public attention, it must also be underlined that the use of alcohol can result in a host of other physical, social, and mental disabilities in addition (Chapter 5). Anyone suffering from the syndrome in severe degree is likely to incur serious alcohol-related disabilities and, because of diminished ability to modify his drinking in the face of such punishing experience, he will go on incurring more and more harm. To this extent the dependence syndrome and disability march hand-in-hand – it is almost impossible to imagine someone who is severely dependent and who has not incurred health or social disabilities as a result of his drinking.

However, the reverse does not necessarily hold. It is frequently the case that an individual who is not alcohol dependent nonetheless uses alcohol in such a way as to damage himself. It would be entirely insufficient to view the problem which this substance sets society exclusively in terms of the number of people suffering from dependence (and the count of their disabilities). Such a limited focus has in the past often handicapped

8

society's appraisal of the problem confronting it: as a result of a too-narrow concern with dependence, it has been forgotten that alcohol to a greater or lesser extent has adverse impact on the lives of many other people. What is needed is an awareness of the great range of difficulties which may result from drinking, of the undramatic as well as the dramatic damage. We need to grasp the importance of the many forms of damage to health and to social functioning caused by heavy drinking – whether or not the individual has become dependent on alcohol, and without either disregarding or over-emphasizing dependence where it exists. In strict logic, the dependence syndrome might itself best be seen as one very particular type of disability.

At this point it may be useful to give two excerpts from illustrative case histories:

(a) A man aged fifty lost control of his car when drunk and crashed into a lamp-post. He had certainly incurred *disabilities* – he lost his licence, and broke his leg. The history revealed however that he only drank occasionally, but had that evening gone out to dinner with friends and drunk unaccustomedly much. He was not suffering from the dependence syndrome, although as a consequence of his drinking he nearly killed himself and might well have killed someone else.

(b) Another man aged fifty was on the same night stopped by the police because he was driving slowly and with over-elaborate caution. He was found to have a grossly elevated blood alcohol level, and was after prosecution duly disqualified from driving. He had in fact been disqualified on two previous occasions (and had also been involved in one nasty accident of the hit-and-run variety). If a doctor examined him, this man would be found to have a severely enlarged liver. His wife had left him because of his drinking. He was severely dependent on alcohol and was persistently drinking more than a bottle of whisky each day. He was unable to modify or control his drinking, which increasingly threatened disaster.

In terms of the thinking of this Report, *both* these men were manifesting behaviour that should have been of the gravest concern to themselves, and to society. To be unconcerned about the first man because he was not alcohol dependent would be to close our eyes to what in sum may be enormously important consequences of drink to society. A story such as the second man gives is however also of great importance. No good is served by arguing which man's story is more or less worrying – the implications of *both* these stories must be of concern.

Alcoholism

This term has been used variously by different people and groups. The fact that much uncertainty attaches to the word is an additional reason for adopting the terms 'dependence' and 'disability'. For most people *alcoholism* is perhaps synonymous with the alcohol dependence syndrome or 'the disease of alcoholism', and this is probably its usage by Alcoholics Anonymous. For others the term has much more inclusive meaning, embracing every type of instance where someone is incurring serious or persistent disability as a result of his drinking, irrespective of dependence. It is in this inclusive sense that we shall use the word *alcoholism* in this Report.

We believe that some better agreement on how words in this area are to be used would serve not only professional people and administrators, but also the man in the street, the writer of radio or TV programmes, and the audience who listens to those programmes. Any terms we adopt today may well be in need of revision in five or ten years' time.

For whom this Report is intended

This Report is intended for everyone who has concern with one of the major health and social problems which confronts this and many other nations. As our Report will show, it is a fundamental misunderstanding of the nature of the disorder to suppose that it can simply be handed over to doctors and social workers. The people who must share in this concern are the mass of ordinary citizens, as well as a wide range of professionals, and those whose work calls on them to implement local and national policy. The Report is deliberately written in non-technical language, to make it intelligible to the widest possible general readership, as well as to people in the professions that have a part to play. To find a style of expression that will suit the layman as well as the specialist is notoriously difficult, but if a report is concerned with basic issues rather than with technical details which are strictly the professional's remit, we believe a common language is possible. For example, the Report will not seek to deal with technical details of treatment such as the choice of drug to combat withdrawal symptoms, or the staffing ratio of an in-patient unit, but it will on the other hand be concerned to test basic assumptions regarding who is to be considered 'a suitable case for treatment', or what treatment may achieve.

Part of the intention of the Report is therefore to ask questions, to test assumptions, and to tackle confusions. It aims to inform, and to provide the essential facts on which discussion can be based. Its intention is also to make proposals for a better response to meet these problems – and, as has already been stressed, we believe that what has to be done is the business of that very wide readership which we hope to engage in the necessary debate.

Of course we do not believe that there are suddenly, today, some new and fundamental insights or miraculous technologies which, if properly applied, would at a stroke eliminate a problem that has baffled society for centuries. The Report is intended for those who want no easy comfort nor spurious slogans but who believe that something better has to be done, and that better actions often require not only compassion and determination but clarity in ideas.

2

New awareness

Twenty years ago in this country, alcoholism was largely regarded either as a Music Hall joke or as a disgrace. It was seen as something which did not have much to do with our own century, and a condition from which the British were, by grace of national temperament, deemed to be immune. The indifference of the general public was matched by lack of interest among the professions: medical schools taught only about the physical complications of advanced alcohol abuse; the NHS made no special provisions for treatment; and there was no special nursing or social work interest. Government departments saw no need for action. The nation's drinking problems were passively ignored or purposely denied.

From such neglect, over a comparatively short time alcoholism has become news (albeit with the story often rather muddled). To point to this change in no way implies the complacent assumption that the days of denial and evasion are totally over. The growth of British efforts and awareness has taken place within the context of wider, international changes. From the 1950s onwards, the World Health Organization has urged that drinking problems should receive government attention. Expert opinion in Britain was beneficially influenced by work carried out in many other countries.

The larger part of this chapter seeks to outline the advances of the last twenty-five years, while the final section deals with some present dilemmas and confusions which are increasingly seen to be in need of clarification. The reason for charting out both the achievements and the dilemmas is that without some sense of recent history it is difficult to understand at all fully the exact nature of society's extraordinarily complex responses to, and attitudes towards, its drinking and its drinking problems. Without such understanding, it would be impossible sensibly to plot any course for the future.

New help for the individual

Developments within the National Health Service

In most parts of the country, if an alcoholic had presented himself to his GP in 1950, the family doctor would probably not have felt personally competent to undertake treatment, and there would have been a stark lack of places to which to refer the patient for specialist help. There were a few exceptions, but most often that alcoholic would have had to take his chances in terms of an admission to a general ward of a mental hospital, where he would frequently have been far from welcome and might have found his condition little understood. A significant development took place when, in the early 1950s, the first specialized NHS alcoholism treatment unit in England was established, at Warlingham Park. The work of this unit helped to win the National Health Service over to the belief that alcoholism treatment was a feasible NHS responsibility. In the early 1960s the first Scottish unit was set up in Edinburgh, and in Wales a unit opened in Cardiff. In 1962 a circular was issued by the Ministry of Health which recommended the setting up of a specialized treatment unit in each region. To date, twenty-three such units have been put into operation. Medical work on alcoholism though, has by no means been limited to the specialized units.

Among other influences contributing to new awareness was Alcoholics Anonymous (AA). Despite the anonymity of its individual members, AA began to capture public interest and sympathy. The simple message that alcoholism was an illness, and the optimistic declaration that this illness could be 'arrested', helped to overcome the popular stereotypes and pessimism. A recent community survey found that almost 50 per cent of the people interviewed named AA as a prime source of help for people with drinking problems. In this country, psychiatric hospitals and Alcoholics Anonymous have worked in fruitful partnership, with much two-way referral.

With over 1,000 groups in Great Britain, and a growth rate of approximately 15 per cent per year, Alcoholics Anonymous has ensured that in every city and in most towns an alcoholic can turn to the 'phone book and make contact with help, probably within the hour. In addition to the immediacy of help, AA provides a continuity of support which so many alcoholics find invaluable. A recent national survey showed that most members go to an average of two meetings per week and are involved in a whole range of both formal and informal AA activities. One of the spin-offs from AA is that this fellowship has provided the model for many self-help organizations which now attempt to aid people who are perplexed by other types of personal problem. Alanon (the organization for family members and friends of alcoholics) has been important in providing help for families and developing an awareness that alcoholism is often a family problem. Al-Ateen offers support to the teenage children of alcoholics.

The homeless alcoholic

The problem of the homeless alcoholic has been a traditional concern of the Salvation Army and the churches, and of voluntary organizations in general. But until recently the chronic inebriate lying out on a derelict site or the drunk begging at the street corner would often be regarded more as a public nuisance than as an alcoholic deserving help. He would appear repeatedly before a magistrate for a sentence of 'ten bob or a day' and, when not sleeping rough, circulated between doss-house and prison. He was a symbolic figure of society's uncaringness and denial – an ugly embarrassment, rather than a human being. Even some of those who began to take a medical interest in alcoholism tended perhaps at first to see him as 'a drunk' rather than 'a real alcoholic', and disdained him as someone who would reinforce the worst stereotypes and get alcoholism a bad name. In 1961 St Luke's House in Lambeth was set up as an alcoholism hostel by the West London Mission and provided a prototype for the specialized rehabilitation centre. Other hostel experiments soon followed, with Rathcoole House (in Clapham), providing an early example of work with drinkers who were ex-offenders.

The Home Office Committee on the Treatment of the Chronic Drunkenness Offender within the Penal System reported in 1971, and recommended that a system of care and rehabilitation should be substituted for the traditional penal handling. It proposed the setting up of Detoxification Centres to which the inebriate would be taken, rather than having him locked up in the police cell. The report also proposed expansion in specialized hostels, 'shop-front' counselling centres, and other social work facilities. That a government committee could report in this way must again be seen in terms of symbolic significance as well as substance: society was declaring that alcoholism was society's business, and that old evasions and denials of responsibility could no longer serve. There have, however, been great delays in seeing the report's recommendations implemented on any sizable scale. Responsibility for implementing those recommendations now lies largely with the Department of Health and Social Security (DHSS) and local authorities, working in conjunction with voluntary organizations. A DHSS circular on community services for alcoholism, which had its primary bearing on services for the homeless alcoholic, was issued in 1973. The first pilot Detoxification Centres are now in operation.

Educating the professionals

Another change has been in the improvement of professional education on alcoholism, although the extent to which the situation has been remedied should not be exaggerated. The Medical Council on Alcoholism, set up in 1967, has been concerned with the development of medical education on alcoholism. For instance, one-day seminars have been held in London and Edinburgh for medical students from around the country. Influence has been brought to bear by preparation of teaching material, the Council's *Journal on Alcoholism* is sent without charge to medical practitioners, and medical conferences have been organized. Taken singly such activities and events may sound no more exciting than a listing in an Annual Report, but taken together they represent one way in which change in professional attitudes is being brought about slowly, and professional ignorance and indifference diminished.

The Alcohol Education Centre (AEC) is another organization involved with professional education, and in this instance not only with the education of medical doctors but of all other professionals whose work may bring them into contact with the alcoholic: nurses, social workers, probation officers, and prison officers, to name only a few special groups. Since 1969 a series of annual residential Summer Schools on Alcoholism have been held, at first run by the Camberwell Council on Alcoholism. In 1972 funding was obtained from the DHSS to support a centre specifically concerned with education, and hence the AEC came into being. The Centre has taken up its brief energetically: not only does the Summer School continue, but during 1977 a total of fifty-one courses for various special professional groups were held up and down the country. The annual enrolment of students in summer schools and other courses combined now totals about 3,000, and the impact goes far beyond these numbers because many of those taught will themselves become teachers.

Building the community's own awareness

The special units and AA essentially promoted a vision of a solution in terms of treating the individual who was already a more-or-less extreme casualty, and placing the responsibility on the specialist or on a specialized organization. As has already been argued, the community may by inference come to feel itself excused from its own responsibilities – the problem is simply about a few ill people, and they can be left to the illness agencies. The events which purposely or accidentally have moved the community itself towards greater awareness will be considered next.

Local Councils on Alcoholism and the National Council on Alcoholism

In 1961 the first moves were made to set up a local Council on Alcoholism in a London borough, and in 1962 the National Council on Alcoholism came into being as a voluntary organization dedicated to fostering the setting up of local Councils across the country. So far in England and Wales, with a similar number functioning in Scotland under the auspices of the Scottish Council on Alcoholism, about twenty such Councils have been established. In part these Councils have simply contributed another element to the spectrum of available help for the individual, and the Alcoholism Information Centres which they run have provided help for the alcoholic and the family. The Councils have also taken responsibility for education within the community, for meeting the special problems of alcoholism in industry, for running courses and seminars, and for urging the better provision of help. At best, their activity can mean that a community realizes and meets some of its own responsibilities – Rotary knows where to find a speaker, the Mayor is the Council's vice-president, the local newspaper takes a sympathetic interest, the alcoholic is no longer quite so disdained, money is found for a hostel, and the local MP asks a useful question in Parliament.

The liquor licensing reports as stimulus to debate

Debate on the health implications of alcohol consumption has also been stirred up by two important government reports on liquor licensing – the *Erroll Report* for England and Wales issued in 1972, and the *Clayson Report* for Scotland, published in 1973. Government impingement on the citizen's drinking, in terms of liquor taxation, the licensing of premises, 'permitted hours', and so on, has a venerable history. The motives behind these government measures have been various. Taxation has traditionally been the Chancellor's business, a weapon wielded in terms of budgetary rather than health interests. Licensing, on the other hand, has its origins in official concern for public order, if not for public health. The general shape of the present licensing laws still owes much to acute anxiety in the period 1914–18 with regard to the impact of drunkenness on the war effort. That the Government should in the 1970s have set up committees on licensing both for England and Wales, and for Scotland, did not signal some new official awareness of the health implications of drinking; the exercises were intended to do no more than meet the routine periodic need for tidying up enactments which had grown piecemeal over the years. Both committees recommended relaxation in controls. In the event, what was to be historically important about these committees was the unforeseen vigour of medical reaction to their recommendations. Both the *British Medical Journal* and the *Lancet* produced editorials attacking proposals which were condemned as contrary to the interests of health. The relationship between normal drinking patterns and the country's experience of alcohol-related casualties was accidentally but unequivocally put into the arena of debate.

Drunken driving as everybody's business

In the context of community awareness, the particular importance of the drunken driving issue was that it began to raise questions, not about the clinically recognizable alcoholic or the 'Skid Row' drunk, but about the social implications of the ordinary

18

citizen's own drinking. In this instance it was not the professional who had to be educated on how to treat the alcoholic, but the citizen who drove a car who had to be taught about the implications of his personal drinking behaviour. Drunken driving was of vital importance as an example of an issue which forced an awareness that the nation's drinking problem could not be tidied away, and was not merely about 'patients', while the rest of us remained happily uninvolved.

The *Road Safety Act* of 1967 introduced the use of the breath-alyzer. Proposals for random breath testing were unacceptable to Parliament. Change in public awareness of the seriousness of the hazards caused by drunk driving is however indicated by polls conducted by the Automobile Association on the acceptability of random breath testing. In 1968, 25 per cent of a sample polled were in favour of random testing, and 68 per cent against such testing. By 1975 the balance of committed opinion had swung the other way – 48 per cent were in favour, and 37 per cent against. A government report on drunken driving, issued in 1976, proposed a general tightening of legislation and received a favourable press. The drunken driving issue in its wider aspects is dealt with more fully in a later chapter (see pp. 68–73).

The Health Education Council and the Scottish Health Education Unit

Recently two government-backed bodies, the Health Education Council and the Scottish Health Education Unit, have played a role in public education on alcoholism. At a cost of £100,000, an extensive campaign was mounted in 1975 in the north-east of England, with the use of spot television messages. Although it seems unlikely that a relatively short-term campaign can produce more than an extremely transient shift in fundamental attitudes, there is no doubt that the campaign was successful in persuading large numbers of people who were worried about their drinking to seek help. But quite apart from the effectiveness of the campaign, what needs to be noted is the importance of such a happening as a socially significant event in its own right. That the Health Education Council was willing to devote such a slice of public money to this effort indicates great changes from the inertia of the 1950s. A further campaign is now under way.

Impact of the mass media

Whatever the activities of professionals, or councils or committees, or government departments or international agencies, the total impact on the awarenesses of the man and woman in the street would have been only slight had it not been for the fact that, at some point during the last ten years or so, drinking and drinking problems became newsworthy. The daily press has carried relevant news reports and feature articles, Sunday supplements have devoted space to alcohol problems, women's magazines discuss the wife's dilemmas, and radio and television have on many occasions produced programmes on alcoholism, occasionally trivial, but more often serious and informative.

Backing for research

The degree to which a country is willing to back research into a particular problem is often an indication of the seriousness with which that problem is being viewed. In the 1950s research spending in Britain on alcoholism was minimal. It was only in the 1960s that the Medical Research Council (MRC) and the Ministry of Health (and later the DHSS), began to provide substantial backing for research in this field. Evidence of changed attitudes was a statement in the MRC's 1976 Report that alcoholism studies were to be considered one of the Council's priority areas. In Scotland, the Chief Scientist's office has recently been active in promoting research into drinking and alcoholism. On a smaller scale, the Medical Council on Alcoholism has funded a number of important projects, and provided Research Fellowships, while the Scottish Council on Alcoholism similarly backs research.

The DHSS Advisory Committee:
alcoholism officially arrived

A symbolic stamp of official concern was the setting up in 1975 of a DHSS Advisory Committee on Alcoholism. This brought together representatives of a wide variety of professions and organizations with an interest in alcoholism and Civil Servants from the DHSS and other government departments. The major work of the committee is carried out in its subcommittees, whose job it is not only to deliberate but to produce reports which deal with a range of topics including prevention, treatment services, provision of help for the homeless alcoholic, and professional education. A remarkable change in concern can certainly be inferred from the setting up of an Advisory Committee by a government department in which, some twenty years earlier, hardly anyone had given alcoholism a thought.

Confusions and dilemmas

Here we shall set out a few issues which are fundamental to the debates that have been stirred up by the recently increased interest in alcoholism. In later sections of the Report it will be necessary to return to some of these questions in greater detail.

A confusion of models

Interwoven with many other issues are the *models of understanding* which are employed when alcohol problems are defined, attitudes to them formed, policies designed, and actions taken. The ideas which produce the actions may not have been consciously formulated, but their importance can be illustrated by such a practical decision as whether the next person drunk in public goes to prison or to hospital, or what we say (or do not say) to the next drunk person leaving a party to climb into his car. The issue no longer lies simply in a choice between the old extremes of a badness or a sickness model, for a variety of models seem to be concurrently and rather inconsistently in use. Drinking, whether normal or excessive, can be seen simply as *social behaviour*, as

21

something to be explained within sociological or anthropological concepts. Drinking can be seen in terms of an *economic* model, where alcohol becomes a commodity manufactured, marketed, and sold. An *educational* model is probably also in operation: drinking is learnt manners, prevention suggests the need for better education on how to drink, and treatment is in essence remedial education. Such an approach is in some ways close to a *psychological* model which analyses learning processes and offers behaviour therapies, but some alternative psychological approaches would explain drinking and abnormal drinking as *coping mechanism*, would look for the role of alcohol in *tension reduction*, and make much of *individual differences in personality*. The *psychiatric and medical* models certainly borrow from many other disciplines and there is no one 'medical model': alcoholism can occur as an accompaniment of neurosis or personality disorder, or mental illness, but it is certainly no part of the current medical approach to propose that such disorders invariably underlie excessive drinking. There is no intrinsic harm in having more than one model available, and it would be premature to insist that there is only one way to think about drinking and excessive drinking. But the confusion becomes harmful when models are only half worked out and their inferences too clumsily drawn; when competing models are inappropriately mixed together; or when people think they are operating on the same assumptions but are in fact radically misunderstanding each other. As much might be said for society's approach to many other complexities, for example in the field of criminology, but alcoholism shows these confusions in extreme form.

Multiple origins

The temptation has always been to look for 'the' explanation of excessive drinking. In terms of popular theorizing it is all due to slum conditions; or it is a symptom of too much affluence; or the stress of modern living provides the explanation; or alcoholism is due to bad homes and faulty child rearing; or it all stems from the drinker's personality; or perhaps alcoholics are born rather than made, and genetics hold the answer. What has to be realized is that causes of excessive drinking are always multiple and interactive, and that any single-factor model of causation is not only wrong in theory, but in practice will lead to inappropriate responses to the individual, and to imperfect social policies.

Delineating the cause for concern

Is society to be compassionately concerned with casually excessive drinking which leads to drunken brawls, marital disharmony, time lost from work on Monday morning, a fall down stairs, a crashed car – or is the new concern only with 'real alcoholics', while all these other happenings are dismissed as not quite anyone's business, or certainly not within the remit of any discussion on alcoholism? We have already touched on this problem in discussing the definition of terms (pp. 7–10), and inherent in this Report is, as we have suggested, the belief that any and all disabilities resulting from excessive drinking are of concern to society.

The implications of calling alcohol a 'drug'

How can this rather frightening and perhaps derogatory label be correctly attached to a substance that most people use all their adult lives without being aware of any lure to addiction? This question receives close attention in Chapters 3 and 4.

The level at which the nation drinks and the level of the country's drinking problems

Until recently, the traditional view would have been that however much or little was drunk by the average citizen, a few people would be fated to become alcoholics, without the general level of the country's drinking having any bearing on the unhappy fate of this fixed minority. Cheaper alcohol, and relaxed licensing hours, would add to the safe pleasures of the ordinary drinker but would not add to the sum of casualties. The sharp distinction between the determinants of ordinary drinking and harmful drinking has, in recent years, been challenged by a mass of research, and central to many of the arguments of this Report is a belief that the evidence shows conclusively that a country's level of drinking has an important influence on that country's level of harm from drinking (Chapter 6).

The recognition of trouble in practical terms

There has been a drive to tell people that alcoholism is an illness which should be treated early, and yet the housewife who hears that message on her radio may still be confused as to whether she, or her son, or her husband, really has a problem which requires outside help. Definition is not a philosophical but an eminently practical question for the worried individual, and the available guidelines may seem confused. Have I got a problem if I cannot do without a sherry in the evening? Is it true that I am at risk if I like to have a few drinks to get into the mood before going to a party? Have I really got a problem if I drink a bottle of whisky a day, given that I can almost certainly comfort myself by referring to someone who is drinking a bottle-and-a-half each day? Such queries deserve to be met, and the stance taken by this Report is quite simply that a person has a drinking problem if his drinking is causing him any sort of harm or causing harm to any other person, and this has to be the immediate question tested by anyone raising this query. But beyond this first question it is also important that the person who raises this query should be given explicit information on the symptoms which allow recognition of the dependence syndrome, whether in its incipient, developed, or more advanced stages (pp. 40–5).

Is alcoholism a treatable condition, or is the outlook pretty hopeless?

There is much uncertainty as to how this question should be answered honestly, and it is one which is repeatedly asked not only by the patient and his family, but by the GP who wonders whether it is worth his while trying to help or to refer; by the employer who wonders whether there is something more constructive to be done than sack his drunken employee; and by the

24

judge who would like to find a constructive alternative to punishment. The simple and quite certain answer is that people whose drinking is harming them can often be helped, but help does not necessarily mean specialized treatment. Such people can indeed often help themselves. However, it only adds to the confusion to quote, as if it were absolute, this or that percentage 'for treatment success in alcoholism': 'treatment', 'alcoholism', and 'success' are each very complicated ideas. These questions will be taken up again in Chapter 7.

The balance between prevention and treatment

Prevention is always preferable to cure, but on the other hand it has proved difficult to stop people from smoking cigarettes. Is the present pattern of government response, which gives much more attention and more money to treatment services for alcoholism than to prevention, soundly based? This question is taken up again in Chapter 8.

These then are some of the old and new questions which now come into focus. They certainly cannot all be answered confidently and immediately, but if society rushes headlong past these difficult issues and ignores them, then confusion is likely to be made even worse. The price of beer comes down, in real terms, and we know this is dangerous for the nation's health: a Minister refers beer to the Prices Commission because he thinks it is too expensive. A patient is turned away from a treatment centre because he is not 'a real alcoholic': the court makes treatment a condition of probation. In high places and in ordinary situations the underlying confusions in ideas express themselves time and again, leading to confusion in large and small happenings.

3

Alcohol and its
immediate effects

Introduction

What is so often left out of any discussion about alcoholism is any
consideration of the nature of *alcohol* itself. Society engages in
widespread use of a drug with potent, varied, and complex
actions, while giving hardly so much as a thought to the actual
nature of that substance. Before this Report looks at the damages
which can result from excessive drinking and examines its causes,
a chapter will therefore be devoted to the nature of alcohol, and
its short-term effects on human beings.

Many different substances are known to the chemist as alcohols, but almost all are so toxic that they are unsuitable for
human consumption. The major exception is ethyl alcohol,
which has the chemical formula C_2H_5OH. Pure ethyl alcohol
(ethanol) is a colourless, inflammable liquid with a characteristic
but weak smell and a strong burning taste. This seemingly un-
remarkable combination of carbon, hydrogen, and oxygen has
been the basis of all commonly used intoxicating beverages since
at least 6,000 B C. Unless otherwise stated it is to *ethyl alcohol* we
refer when talking about *alcohol*.

Production and the varieties of beverage

Alcohol is produced by the action of yeast fungi, which ferment certain sugars to form carbon dioxide and ethyl alcohol. This process continues until the sugar supply is exhausted, or until the alcohol level reaches about 14 per cent by volume, at which concentration the yeast can no longer survive. The production of carbon dioxide is responsible for the 'head' on a glass of beer and the sparkle of champagne. Fermentation was the only method of producing alcohol known to primitive man, but in about 800 AD an Arab known as Jahir ibn Hayyan is said to have developed the art of distillation. This process of boiling and isolating the more volatile alochol from the other fluids allowed the production of much more potent beverages.

Alcoholic drinks consist mainly of ethyl alcohol and water, but most also contain a variety of other substances sometimes called congeners; these include ethyl acetate, iso-amyl alcohol, various sugars, minerals, and B-group vitamins. Their concentrations range from 3 g per 100 litres of vodka to 285 g per 100 litres of bourbon. They contribute to the causes of 'hangover', while tyramine, which is found in wine and some beers, can interact with a particular class of drugs used in treatment of depression (mono-amine oxidase inhibitors) to cause severe headache and acutely raised blood pressure. Congeners probably do not have any other important pharmacological action, but they give the characteristic colour and flavour to different beverages, and in that sense are of great importance to the drinker.

A number of different systems are used to indicate the concentration of alcohol in various drinks, and these cause endless confusion. The most rational is the percentage of alcohol by volume (% v/v). 'Proof' scales are also widely used, particularly for revenue purposes. The notion of 'proof' originated centuries ago when, if gun powder soaked with the beverage burnt on ignition, this was taken as 'proof' that the liquor was more than half alcohol. In the American proof scale, one degree is equal to $\frac{1}{2}$% v/v. As if that were not sufficiently complicated, the British scale is characteristically less straightforward, with 57·15 per cent by volume being designated as 100° proof. Thus, a concentration of alcohol of 43% v/v is equivalent to 86° proof on the American scale and 75° proof on the British scale.

There is an immense variety of alcoholic beverages, but most can be placed in one of five major categories: beers, table wines, dessert or cocktail wines, distilled spirits, and liqueurs. The production and characteristics of these are described in *Table 1*.

In addition to its use as a beverage, alcohol is widely used in industry as a solvent. Industrial alcohol includes absolute alcohol (99·9% v/v), and various additives which aim to make the product undrinkable. Alcohol is also a starting material for chemical products such as acetic acid, lacquers, varnishes, dyes, and artificial fibres.

Absorption and metabolism in the human body

The rate of absorption is influenced by a number of factors. The higher the concentration of alcohol, up to a maximum of 40 per cent by volume, the more rapid its absorption, so that absorption is slower from beers than from spirits. Other chemicals in the beverage can also be of importance – the sugars in sweet drinks retard absorption, while the carbon dioxide and bicarbonate of sparkling wines or of a whisky and soda accelerate absorption. In the case of rapid absorption, a higher peak of alcohol level in the blood is commonly reached; the same quantity of pure alcohol absorbed more slowly will be in the bloodstream for a longer period, but will not reach such a high peak. Food conspicuously delays absorption of alcohol, mainly by slowing the stomach's emptying; taking a meal before a drink may reduce the peak blood alcohol level by almost 50 per cent.

Once alcohol is absorbed into the body through the stomach and the intestines, it is initially distributed through the body by the blood stream; organs such as the liver and brain, which have a rich blood supply, are reached first. In pregnant women, alcohol crosses the placental barrier into the foetus.

In man, only some 2 per cent to 5 per cent of alcohol is eliminated unchanged, via the kidneys and the lungs; although the quantity of alcohol in the air breathed out of the lungs is small,

Table 1 Production and content of alcoholic beverages

Group	Examples of specific beverages	Alcohol content % v/v	Production
Beers	Lager Ales Stout	3–6 3–6 4–8	Brewer's wort fermented by yeast with hops as flavouring
Table wines	Still: red, white, and rosé	8–14	Fermentation of crushed grapes or grape juice.
	Sparkling: champagne	12	Second fermentation with retention of carbon dioxide
Dessert and cocktail wine.	Sherry, port, madeira, vermouth	15–20	Ordinary wines plus added brandy or high proof spirit and plant extracts as flavouring
Distilled spirits	Brandy	40	Direct distillation of fermented grape mash
	Whisky	37–40	Double distillation of fermented barley or corn mash
	Rum	40	Distillation of fermented molasses
	Gin	37–40	Tasteless distillate flavoured by second distillation with berries, etc.
	Vodka	37·5	Distillation of grain
Liqueurs	Benedictine, chartreuse, kirsch	20–55	Neutral spirits plus flavouring

it correlates well with concentrations in the blood and tissues, and thus provides the basis for the breathalyzer test.

Four pints of beer taken by a person of average size might take some four or five hours to be metabolized by the body, and if the amount drunk were doubled it would take roughly twice as long. The rate of metabolism can increase when large amounts of alcohol are drunk, and heavy drinkers usually metabolize alcohol rather more rapidly than light drinkers.

Short-term drug actions

The metabolism of alcohol yields calories and alcohol can thus be considered a food. However, it is generally consumed not for its calorie content but because it changes the drinker's mood and thinking. A drug has been defined as 'Any substance that, when taken into the living organism, may modify one or more of its functions.' Substances that alter an individual's psychological state are known as psychotropic drugs. To describe alcohol simply as a food is to ignore its more important effects, namely its properties as a drug which affects mental functions. The remainder of this chapter will be devoted to describing its pharmacological (drug) effects, in particular its effects on the central nervous system.

General effects

When alcohol is consumed, it exerts minor effects on the circulation of the blood. Moderate doses cause a small, transient increase in heart rate. Although not a general dilator of arteries and therefore without benefit to those with coronary artery disease, it dilates blood vessels in the skin and hence produces its characteristic flush. The flush causes a feeling of warmth, but heat loss from increased sweating may lead to a fall in body temperature. With large doses the temperature-regulating mechanism in the brain itself becomes depressed, and the fall in body temperature may become pronounced. Brandy is therefore far from being a specific against exposure to cold as popularly imagined.

Alcohol is inadvisable for those with stomach or duodenal

ulcers not only because drinks of 40 per cent concentration and over cause inflammation of the stomach lining, but also because it is an effective stimulus to the production of gastric juices and acids which make the ulcer worse.

Although the large volume of fluid ordinarily ingested with alcohol is the main cause of increased urine flow, alcohol produces a more direct effect on physiological mechanisms controlling production of urine.

Because of its relatively rapid evaporation at body temperatures, alcohol applied externally causes cooling of the skin. Direct application of higher concentrations can slightly injure body cells, and hence the stinging sensation on the lining of the mouth caused by spirits. Alcohol also possesses a valuable local antiseptic action, but this occurs optimally at concentrations much higher than those of alcoholic drinks.

Effects on the brain

The effect of alcohol on the functioning of the nervous system is, of course, the main reason for its widespread consumption. The brain is more markedly affected by alcohol than any other system in the body but, contrary to the layman's view, alcohol is in the true sense a depressant of the nervous system. Stimulant properties have popularly been attributed because individuals under its influence often become talkative, aggressive, and hyperactive. This apparent stimulation is better described as disinhibition, and arises from the unrestrained activity of parts of the brain freed from the inhibitory control of other centres, and also very importantly the way the culture and the immediate environment suggests that an intoxicated person should actually behave.

While the exact mechanisms of the action of alcohol remain controversial, we do know that its effects are dependent on dosage. The first consistent changes in mood and behaviour appear at blood levels of about 50 mg %, at which level the majority of individuals feel carefree and released from many of their ordinary anxieties and inhibitions. As the blood alcohol rises, progressively more functions of the brain are affected. Driving skill is affected at 30 mg % and seriously affected by 80 mg %.

Clumsiness and emotional lability follow at a level of 100 mg %, and at 200 mg % those parts of the brain which control movement and emotional behaviour are obviously impaired. At a concentration of 300 mg %, 90 per cent of individuals are very grossly intoxicated. Confusion and then 'passing out' and progressive stupor follow, and the fatal concentration lies between 500 mg % and 800 mg %.

Sensory effects, and effects on movements and co-ordination

Focussing and the ability to follow objects with the eyes are greatly impaired even by low doses of alcohol. Sharpness of vision is relatively insensitive to alcohol. However, at high doses sensitivity to certain colours, especially red, appears to decrease and the ability to discriminate between lights of different intensity is impaired. Recovery from the effect of exposure to glare is delayed. As with vision, the ability to hear sounds remains intact, but discrimination is impaired. Even low doses impair sensitivity to odours and taste, and diminish sensitivity to pain.

Tests of reaction time almost all show that alcohol has a detrimental effect at blood levels above 50 mg %, but show no consistent effects at lower concentrations. Greater complexity of a task increases alcohol's adverse effects, and speed tests requiring sustained responses to complex stimuli are most affected. The relevance to drunken driving is obvious. The person who is an experienced drinker may show less impairment in test performance on certain tasks than the naive drinker, but it would be entirely wrong to suppose that tolerance is ever more than partial, and the belief that a heavy drinker can 'handle his liquor' is to a great extent a dangerous myth.

Effects on complex intellectual functions

Performance on standard intellectual tests show the substantial adverse effects of moderate or even small doses of alcohol. Memory for words, fluency in their use, and the quality of word association are all impaired. When alcohol is consumed in a social setting communication becomes more disorganized, and the conventional rules of speech etiquette may be flouted. Drinkers break into their partners' conversations more frequently, and their responses show less knowledge of what their partners are talking about.

Fine tests of discrimination, of memory, and of arithmetical ability show that impairment begins at low blood alcohol levels, although with arithmetic accuracy is affected more than speed. Interestingly, things learned while intoxicated may be recalled better during a similar state than when sober. And although high doses of alcohol undoubtedly impair ability to solve problems, low doses may occasionally help solve difficult and unfamiliar problems, perhaps through a greater willingness to try unusual lines of thinking.

The more alcohol is drunk, the more judgement is lost. Unfortunately, many people under the influence of alcohol believe that their performance is normal, or even improved. Alcohol thus tends to increase risk taking. Bus drivers given several drinks were shown to be more likely to try to drive their buses through spaces that were too small. In simulated driving tests, extroverts tend to react to alcohol by making more mistakes but not altering speed, while introverts tend to reduce speed and make fewer errors. Normally anxious individuals appear better able to compensate for the effects of alcohol. Pain, exertion, and cold enhance the ability of drinkers to 'pull themselves together' although compensation will be very far from complete. The benefits of the traditional black coffee are very slight.

Effect on mood

As has already been mentioned, the pharmacological effect of alcohol on mood is difficult to disentangle from the circumstances in which the alcohol is taken, and the effect which the drinker *expects* drinking to have. It has been suggested that the surrounding circumstances produce greater change than the alcohol itself. Among the contributing factors are the mood of the occasion, the personality of the drinker, whether the drinker is alone or with others, and the sex of the drinker and any companions.

Nevertheless, when subjects are experimentally given alcohol, the observed alterations in mood largely confirm everyday experience. Such subjects frequently appear disinhibited and less afraid of situations which normally provoke fear. Moods commonly reported include greater contentment, cheerfulness, and euphoria, but these pleasant moods may suddenly change to acute unhappiness or aggression. Exhilarated feelings are much enhanced in convivial, social settings such as a pub, and as any party-giver knows alcohol decreases social anxiety and promotes sociability. After a few drinks conversation appears to sparkle, dull people seem more interesting, and feeble jokes funny.

Some studies have shown an increase in the uninhibited expression of sexual behaviour and self-assertion. Alcohol is widely thought to be an aphrodisiac, but this is not strictly true. A few drinks dull the sense of restraint and can help to overcome shyness, lack of confidence, or feelings of inferiority and guilt regarding sex, but large doses spoil the capacity to perform.

The disinhibiting effects of alcohol may release suppressed feelings of aggression and hostility. Numerous investigations have associated intoxication with impulsive violence. Not only do people get involved in more arguments and accidents when 'under the influence', but assaults are also more frequent.

Interactions with other drugs

Alcohol is a powerful pharmacological agent which may interact with other drugs. Such interactions are most likely to occur following continuous heavy drinking, but even moderate drinking may constitute a risk with some medicines. Some commonly seen drug-alcohol interactions can be predicted on the basis of the known pharmacological properties of alcohol. For example, since alcohol is a central nervous system depressant, it may strengthen the effects of sedatives including the barbiturates and minor tranquillizers such as Librium and Valium. When an overdose of barbiturates is taken in combination with alcohol, the resulting coma may be deeper and more dangerous.

A number of drugs, including several oral anti-diabetic agents, can inhibit the breakdown of alcohol, and cause the accumulation of acetaldehyde, with resulting nausea, vomiting, headache, and falling blood pressure. A controlled form of this reaction using disulfiram (Antabuse) has been employed as a form of 'chemical fence' around alcoholics in treatment.

The speed of breakdown of some drugs is dependent on liver enzymes which are also involved in the metabolism of alcohol. When the two are taken together they 'compete' for the same enzymes, and the action of the drug may be increased because of its slower breakdown; thus, individuals taking the anti-coagulant Warfarin who have an acute drinking bout may precipitate bleeding. On the other hand, the consumption of large quantities of alcohol over prolonged periods can lead to these same enzymes becoming superefficient. Thus, prolonged heavy drinking doubles the rate at which the anti-epileptic drug phenytoin (Epanutin) is broken down, and may, therefore, threaten the control of epilepsy.

Alcohol as a drug

Whenever anyone takes a drink containing alcohol, it must by now be clear that the consequence is a vastly complex set of interactions between a drug and that individual's body (particularly his brain). What has to be inferred from even a brief review of the fundamental nature of ethyl alcohol is the simple message that alcohol is a drug, and not an inert substance or something to be taken into the body as casually as a glass of water. The bigger the dose, the greater the effects. It is a drug that interacts with other drugs.

To call alcohol 'a drug' may to the ordinary drinker at first seem to propose an odd and perhaps a rather unacceptable way of looking at the familiar pint of beer or glass of sherry. For that person the symbolism of the word 'drug' may suggest either a substance used in medicine, or a narcotic whose misuse is associated with addiction. The plain truth is that alcohol is in fact a drug among drugs: it is closely similar in many of its actions to substances used in medicine, and it does have the potential to induce addiction. The drinker may happily continue with his pint or with her sherry, but the drinker and society need much greater

35

awareness of the fact that our culture is making the decision to co-exist with the use, for fun and recreation, of a drug which is as powerful and complex in its actions as many substances which are available only on prescription.

People should know about the calorie and protein value and health consequences of the food they eat, and every ordinary person can take an intelligent interest in his diet without spoiling the enjoyment of the next meal. We are courting danger if we excuse ourselves from an understanding of the drug in our diet. The traditional strategy that western society has employed to reduce its anxieties is to pretend that alcohol is not *really* a drug, but that it is a beverage, a pint of this or a bottle of that. The Moslem world has always known otherwise. We should argue that our society's needs and the safety of its continued co-existence with alcohol must today be better served by a wider knowledge and admission of the true facts.

4

Alcohol dependence

Society needs to come to a full awareness that disabilities from alcohol not only affect that small proportion of people who are addicted to alcohol, but that the damage is spread much more widely. So much has already been made clear. Having insisted on a wider perspective than has often been shown previously in attitudes about health, the fact remains that at the extreme end of the spectrum there are people who are suffering from a type of involvement with alcohol which requires very special understanding. These are people who have developed the dependence syndrome – who are addicted to, or dependent on, alcohol.

This chapter will therefore look firstly at the general meaning to be given to the idea of drug dependence, and then specifically at the picture of alcohol dependence. Brief note will be taken of present understanding of the biological and psychological basis of this condition. The implications of dependence will then be examined, in terms both of what it means for the individual to be dependent, and the meaning for the family and for the society who have to react to him. How society is to look at the problem will receive this attention because there can be no doubt that the way in which dependence is conceived will greatly influence the way in which society responds. Are we dealing with bad behaviour, or in any real sense with illness or disease?

Drug dependence: the general meaning of terms

The terms used in this field tend to be those recommended by the World Health Organization (WHO). In 1965 the WHO suggested that the concept of dependence could usefully replace the terms *addiction* and *habituation*. Dependence, not specifically on alcohol but on any drug or substance, was to be defined in the following way:

'A state, psychic and sometimes also physical, resulting from the interaction between a living organism and a drug, characterized by behavioural and other responses that always include a compulsion to take the drug on a continuous or periodic basis in order to experience its psychic effects, and sometimes to avoid the discomfort of its absence. Tolerance may or may not be present.'

A distinction was then made between psychological and physical dependence.

Psychological dependence: 'A condition in which a drug produces a feeling of satisfaction and a psychic drive that require periodic or continuous administration of the drug to produce pleasure or to avoid discomfort.'
Physical dependence: 'An adaptive state that manifests itself by intense physical disturbance when the administration of the drug is suspended.'

There is no need here to become too embroiled with the logic and semantics which beset the attempt to maintain a strict distinction between psychological and physical dependence, and the alcohol dependence syndrome described in this chapter obviously has both physical and psychological elements. As already mentioned, we will use the word 'dependence' as synonymous with this syndrome rather than continuing to make anything of the idea of separate psychological and physical types of dependence.

The central message of the 1965 WHO recommendations is straightforward and useful. This message is in essence that dependence conditions should be thought of as a *family* of disorders. Between the syndromes produced by one substance and by another there will be certain dissimilarities, and each type of drug dependence has its individual stamp. But there are also common elements – most notably the 'compulsion to take the drug on a continuous or periodic basis'. Once a person is dependent, and whatever the drug, he has contracted a habit which will be extremely difficult to shed.

The major groupings of the dependencies are: (1) dependence on opium-like drugs (opium, heroin, morphia, and synthetic opiates), (2) dependence on stimulant drugs (cocaine and synthetic stimulants such as amphetamines and certain slimming pills), (3) dependence on nicotine (a major reason for the compulsiveness of tobacco smoking), and (4) dependence on depressant substances, which include sedatives, hypnotics, minor tranquillizers – and alcohol. There is disagreement as to whether cannabis produces a dependence syndrome, and although hallucination-inducing substances such as mescaline and LSD can certainly cause serious problems they are taken on an intermittent basis and do not produce syndromes of dependence.

With none of the potentially dependence-inducing drugs does use of the drug *inevitably* lead to the development of a dependence syndrome. For instance, there are opium smokers in Thailand who smoke only an occasional pipe, and adolescent heroin users in London or New York may use the drug on a number of occasions but give it up before being 'hooked'. Opiates generally have a high dependence liability, and the risk of moving from casual use to dependence is great. Nicotine is similarly dangerous, but there are still some people who can smoke an occasional cigarette on a 'take it or leave it' basis.

The depressant substances cover quite a spectrum of dependence potential; for instance, barbiturates must be regarded as far from safe drugs in this respect. Alcohol will, in our society, be used by most people without development of the dependence syndrome. It is the fact that so many people use alcohol without becoming dependent which causes incredulity when it is stated that alcohol is a true drug of dependence. In this incredulity lies a special danger: it is exactly because alcohol has a relatively low dependence potential that it is easy to overlook the relatively small but very real risk of dependence which is involved.

The alcohol dependence syndrome

Any case history would be misleading if it were taken as adequately representing the great variety of pictures of this syndrome which can develop, each patterned by the individual personality and by that individual's personal and social circumstances. The extracts from two case histories which follow should therefore be read with that warning in mind. They are patients' accounts not of how they came to be dependent (though the second story touches on that question), but of what it is like to be dependent.

Two case histories

A forty-year-old male executive: 'I don't understand it. A happy marriage, two lovely children, successful in my work, and here I am wrecking everything. I get up in the morning feeling sick as death – not just physically sick, but mentally sick. Retching if I try to clean my teeth. Some mornings I'm so shaky I can hardly get downstairs. I don't drink in the house as that would upset my wife. Recently I'll keep a bottle in my briefcase and have a quick drink at the station. I'll always have a drink as soon as I get to the office. Couldn't cope without it. A big drink, and half-an-hour later that sickness has gone. The morning cure. Then it's just regular throughout the day – I'm thinking of drink, planning the next drink, feeling a bit sweaty and tense and getting people out of the room if they're staying too long and getting in the way of the next drink. I expect it adds to a bottle-and-a-half of whisky each day, and never much variation. I don't get drunk. You wouldn't know I'd been drinking now, would you? I hate what's happening, tell myself its stupid, promise my wife that today I'm not going to have more than a couple of drinks. Last summer I stopped completely for the whole of August, but when I came back from holiday I started with just the odd drink and within ten days it was square one.'

A retired woman aged sixty-four: 'I suppose it's loneliness, having too much time on my hands, living by myself. It's since I gave up work four years ago that it's begun to happen. I wouldn't call it a serious problem, but I know it's a problem and I don't want it to get worse. I've always liked a glass of sherry now and then and kept a bottle in the house in case friends dropped round – a bottle might last months though and I'd never drink by myself. Four years ago I found myself looking at that bottle one afternoon and thinking well, it wouldn't hurt to have just *one*. I can remember the occasion exactly. Now I suppose it's two bottles a day, always sherry. Sometimes a bit more, and sometimes for a few days I cut it down. It's a problem that has just crept up on me. I don't like going out with people who don't drink, and there used to be nothing I liked more than an afternoon out shopping with my sister. In the morning I don't have what you'd call a hangover. I feel sort of shaky inside and I wouldn't say my hands were too steady. I let the cat out, make a little rule with myself to have a cup of tea and listen to the news on the radio, do some tidying up, and try not to break my rule and have a drink before 10 am but it's sometimes difficult to hold out. It's all so silly, I can't believe it's me.'

The successful executive prefaces the description of his dependence by saying 'I don't understand' and the retired woman Civil Servant says 'It's all so silly.' As well as describing dependence (of two different degrees), they each describe in their own way a common element of bafflement – a feeling which may indeed be shared by any of us when faced with the picture of dependence. Yet if one takes personal accounts such as these, it is not difficult to identify the outlines of a recognizable clinical condition. That outline picture needs to be better known so that the individual himself will recognize earlier what he is suffering from, and those around him will recognize with what they are dealing.

Common elements

The essential and repeated elements of this picture which need to be identified are seven in number:

(a) *Subjective awareness of compulsion to drink*: The drinker who is suffering from severe withdrawal may very desperately want a drink, while that less dependent woman in our second case history would be distinctly edgy and uneasy as she waited for 10 am: the term 'craving' is often used to describe such experience. Both those people also reported a subjective experience of impaired control over their own drinking, and they could no longer be sure of drinking the way they themselves would consider reasonable, or of stopping drinking once they started. Alcohol is felt to be a *necessity* once drinking is under way, and the person himself may describe his experience by saying that alcohol for him has become 'a drug'. Once he starts drinking, he must go on until he obtains the mental effect that he needs. The subjective feeling of compulsion is difficult to capture in words, but anyone who is a dependent cigarette smoker will be able to empathize when he thinks how the tension and craving mounts if he is deprived of a cigarette.

(b) *Narrowing the drinking repertoire*: The ordinary drinker's consumption will vary from day to day, and week to week. He drinks because of a variety of internal or external cues. The dependent drinker will, as his condition advances, drink increasingly and predominantly in response to the need to relieve or avoid withdrawal symptoms, and his drinking repertoire therefore becomes narrowed. He knows that his daily intake is, say, one-and-a-half bottles of whisky, or three bottles of sherry, and he could probably describe within fairly narrow limits exactly how each day's drinking is routinely scheduled. The more dependent he is, the more stereotyped that schedule will become.

(c) *Primacy of drinking over other activities*: Drinking increasingly takes priority over other activities. At the extreme, drinking becomes the dedicated occupation, with all other life demands a series of optional extras. Drinking for that executive had in effect become more important than family or ambition, and the clue given by the woman who gave up her shopping expeditions can provide insight into the real force of the feelings she was experiencing. Often a patient will confess serious lapses in behaviour, dishonesty, deceptions in personal relationships, evasions of responsibility at work, or as yet undiscovered embezzlement or theft, and it will be clear that he accords drink priority although his social position, his home, or his health, are obviously suffering. Appalling disasters may occur, but drinking takes overriding precedence.

(d) *Altered tolerance to alcohol*: Increased tolerance is shown by the dependent person being able to sustain an alcohol intake and go about his business at blood alcohol levels that would seriously affect or incapacitate the non-tolerant drinker – hence that executive's report that he 'never got drunk'. Such an acquired tolerance for alcohol is often misinterpreted by the drinker as meaning that not much can be wrong, whereas in reality exactly the opposite conclusion should be drawn. The fact that a man can still conduct his business on a daily alcohol intake that would incapacitate the ordinary drinker is not proof of some sort of special strength or immunity, but an important indicator of increasing dependence. It is equally interesting and important that in the later stages of alcohol dependence loss of tolerance occurs. The patient's behaviour then becomes disorganized, although he has by no means had the amount of alcohol he requires. A man who could hold prodigious quantities of drink now falls down in the street: he cannot drink sufficient to produce the inner state he seeks (once perfectly possible) without making himself helpless.

(e) *Repeated withdrawal symptoms*: The common withdrawal symptoms are 'bad nerves', shakiness, sweatiness, and nausea, which occur after a drop in blood alcohol level. Especially important as a withdrawal symptom is the disturbance of mood. The sufferer may be tense, jittery, on edge, and feel awful. It can incapacitate him in that he dreads any social interactions, because he feels so bad in himself. These symptoms may at an earlier stage be only mild, occur perhaps only after a few days of particularly hard drinking, and not all the symptoms may be experienced. At the extreme, withdrawal may result in fully developed delirium tremens, or in major convulsions. Withdrawal is most usually experienced on waking in the morning, but can occur during the day if the heavily dependent person goes too long without a drink. Any circumstance which suddenly leads to reduction of intake or complete abstinence may of course precipitate withdrawal symptoms – admission to hospital because of an accident or arrest and imprisonment are typical circumstances in which delirium tremens may develop.

(f) *Relief or avoidance of withdrawal symptoms by further drinking*: From drinking in order to feel better, the dependent drinker drinks in order to avoid feeling worse. He recognizes his withdrawal symptoms as such: it is not only the severe morning symptoms which have to be 'cured' (he may not be able to do up his shirt-buttons without a drink) but if he is severely dependent he will react to mild symptoms which occur during the day if he goes too long without a drink. The executive tried to get people out of his room when he began to sense these symptoms coming on, so that he could reach the bottle in his desk. It is only when we remember the shame with which many alcohol-dependent people drink and the symptom itself that we are now discussing – the avoidance of withdrawal symptoms by repeated drinking – that we can understand why these people need to hide drink in various accessible places often in much earlier stages of dependence than we credit, and in such a manner that relatives or colleagues do not realize the amount of alcohol they get through. Secrecy, deception, dissimulation about the amount of alcohol taken, and hidden supplies are all related to this necessity to stave off or minimize withdrawal symptoms.

(g) *Reinstatement after abstinence*: The alcohol-dependent

44

person often says that abstinence is surprisingly easy to maintain. The drinker who has been abstinent for a week or two has no craving, and persuades himself that he therefore cannot have any problem, so he starts experimentally to drink again – and hence the story of that August holiday and 'back to square one'. But relapse into the previous degree of dependence can follow a variable course, depending to an extent on the severity of the dependence which that person had previously experienced. The severely dependent person is likely, when he drinks again, to relapse explosively, and to return to his old drinking pattern immediately or within a few days. The mildly dependent person may take weeks or months before he is again experiencing withdrawal, and is then probably moving towards more serious dependence than before.

'Aren't we all dependent?'

A condition must be recognized which exists in degrees, and not only in extreme degree. It has many elements within it, rather than any one key diagnostic feature, and is subtle, variable, shaped by many factors, and conforms to no stereotype. The mistake has been made in the past of sometimes painting the picture in such extreme terms that even that executive would be doubtful as to whether it applied to him, and the sixty-four year-old woman would immediately conclude that 'alcoholism' had nothing to do with her particular story.

The question is indeed often asked whether everyone who drinks is not at least in some minor degree dependent on alcohol – the person who, for instance, would feel deprived if he did not have his evening glass of sherry. In that sense we are all in fact 'dependent' for our ordinary happiness, gratification, and emotional sustenance on a whole range of people, roles, and objects; we are in this sense reliant on family and friends, on our jobs, on our motor cars, our favourite armchair and the television set, and perhaps on a glass of sherry in the evening or a couple of pints of beer every Saturday night. Some degree of 'dependence' on

45

alcohol, if the word is used in that way, certainly comes to be a normal condition, and among normal drinkers there will be a wide range of sensed need for alcohol in terms both of drinking occasions and quantity drunk.

But there should be no confusion. The *dependence syndrome* is a very abnormal condition indeed, and the statement that 'we are all dependent on alcohol in some degree' does not mean that we are all suffering from the dependence syndrome in some degree. This is an important point to make: the reality of that syndrome, its separateness from normal experience, and the force of its implications must be insisted on unambiguously, and the clarity of the message must not be lost in any semantic confusions.

Scientific understanding of the alcohol dependence syndrome

Scientific understanding of alcohol dependence is still incomplete, but in recent years our knowledge has certainly advanced. Why a person becomes dependent is a question which can in the first place be taken as an extension of the question of why people drink at all or drink heavily, and these issues are dealt with in Chapter 6. To develop the dependence syndrome it is necessary for a person to engage in heavy drinking. Usually this has to go on for many years, but there are instances where the syndrome develops more rapidly.

Given the necessary heavy drinking, the process of dependence is then set in train by certain biological changes that take place in the central nervous system. In simple terms what seems to happen is that a defensive response is called into play so that the ability of alcohol to depress the activity of the brain is countered. The process leads at first to increased tolerance. This type of tolerance is a necessary prelude to development of withdrawal symptoms. The processes that have countered depression of brain activity in the presence of alcohol cause a surge of excitation when alcohol is removed. The analogy might be with the door that has a person on one side pushing it, and on the other side someone holding it shut: suddenly stop holding it shut, and the countervailing pushing of the other person now sends the door flying open with great energy.

Such an account of tolerance and withdrawal is immensely oversimplified. What needs to be emphasized is that the processes involved are ultimately susceptible to laboratory analysis, and that we no longer have to regard the biological basis of the dependence syndrome as an unassailable mystery. It is possible that acetalydehyde, one of the break-down products of alcohol, is an active substance in the dependence process.

The next stage is probably that the repeated experience of withdrawal and relief of withdrawal set up a process of conditioning. In these terms alcohol dependence can be seen as *a form of abnormal learning*. In terms of this theory, a person is presumed to learn the compulsiveness of the dependence syndrome's drinking. That a drink can offer avoidance of withdrawal symptoms, as well as actual relief, would theoretically be expected to provide strong additional reinforcement of the habit. It should again be stressed that scientific understanding of the processes involved in dependence is still only provisional, and this is as true with the psychological as with the physiological mechanisms.

These combined biological and learning-theory explanations of dependence appear at first to be abandoning much previous thinking in terms of alcohol dependence as a neurosis, and of the emphasis which has previously been put on the symbolic and psychodynamic meaning of drinking, or on the personality of the drinker, and the influence of the environment. There need in fact be no contradictions. These factors can all be seen as contributory antecedents to the heavy drinking, which then lead to the dependence syndrome. These original factors also continue to be part of the total field even when the psychobiological syndrome of dependence has developed, and are often vitally important aspects in our understanding of the dependent person's total predicament.

Natural history of the alcohol dependence syndrome

A distinction has to be made between the natural history of the core syndrome, and the sequence of personal and social consequences which stem from the condition's progress. Developments along these two lines can first be considered separately, although they are most often rather intimately related. There is enormous variability between individual stories, no absolutely inexorable march of 'phases', but nonetheless there are certain general principles which can aid understanding and allow us to see common elements or processes in seemingly very different case histories.

The evolution of the syndrome

Taking first the question of the natural history of the syndrome itself, what is striking is that patients often seem able to identify fairly closely a crucial period, during which they passed from their own chosen pattern of excessively heavy drinking, to a pattern of drinking that was frighteningly different. This is an account given by a forty-four year-old painter and decorator:

'I've always liked a drink, and in my job there's quite a bit of drinking goes on. I've always earned good money. It was a matter often of a session at lunchtime, and then in the evening I'd usually go down to the local but that wasn't every night. Some days nothing, but that would have been rare, and I wouldn't be too surprised if I'd been averaging eight to ten pints for a good few years. Then three years ago I went up North on this big contract job for nine months, and was living in digs, and getting home perhaps only once a month. That was when things went really bad, and for the first time in my life I was waking up with shakes. Feeling really terrible in the mornings, really rough, but the job had to be done, so it was a quarter bottle of whisky to get me going. The "hair of the dog", you hear about it, but I didn't think that was ever going to be for me. My drinking was really terrible when that job finished

48

but when I was home again I tried to pull out of it and things were better for a week or two. But since then it's really been on top of me, out of control, just not the way it used to be.'

Someone suffering from this syndrome will often draw this immediate distinction between 'the way it used to be' and 'the way it is now', and sensitive questioning will then reveal that the transition has been marked by the emergence, one by one, of the core elements in the dependence syndrome which have been listed and discussed in the previous section.

The idea of a crucial phase of transition raises a number of questions. What variation is there in the abruptness of demarcation? Is it still possible to draw back? What sort of age variation is to be seen in the onset of this phase? How are such variations to be explained?

As regards the abruptness with which 'the way it used to be' can be differentiated from 'the way it is now', there is obviously enormous variation. Some people may reject the idea as not applying at all to their own experience – what is happening to them *now* is perceived just as an extension of what has been happening *all along*. If questioning is directed to the essential elements of the syndrome they may nonetheless be able to perceive that there was in fact a transition, not necessarily in terms of quantity drunk but in terms of ability to control the drinking. Other patients may be able to recognize the onset of the syndrome but will describe the experience not in terms of a precipitous development but as a matter of having experienced a few symptoms, drawn back for six months or a year, gone a little bit nearer the establishment of dependence, and then after a couple more years the syndrome emerging rather rapidly.

The age at which the syndrome becomes established is often the mid-forties for men, and for women perhaps a few years later. But although this is the typical age bracket, the picture can certainly on occasion develop in a patient in his late teens (and this is becoming more common), or emerge for the first time after the age of retirement.

The reasons for the variability in the abruptness of onset and the age of occurrence are multiple. The basic drinking pattern in which the person has been engaging is certainly important: the heavier and more continuous the drinking, the sooner he will become dependent. The individual who is generally rather troubled in his personality will reach an advanced state of dependence more quickly than the more mature and controlled personality, and will sometimes crash through the transitional phase and establish severe dependence with surprising abruptness. Sometimes particular events or life circumstances do much to explain the rapidity and timing – the painter's working away from home, a depressive illness, a sudden legacy, the breakdown of a marriage, working abroad where alcohol is cheap and social patterns invite heavy drinking, bereavement, a worrying period at work, or perhaps just an accumulation of life stresses. One can think both of forces which can push people more or less rapidly towards dependence, and barriers which may slow down the emergence of dependence.

Once the dependence syndrome has been established, it seems to have an impetus of its own, and to progress. A man who was for instance having mild morning shakes regularly two years ago will probably today be having more severe shakes; it is unlikely that the symptoms will have faded away. There is variation but also (unless something is done about the problem) a fair measure of inevitability about the march of events: the natural tendency is for the syndrome to progress, rather than to remit. However, instances do certainly occur in which the drinker regains control of his drinking: such 'control' is usually a pretty precarious and impermanent affair, but the occurrence of true instances of remission must be accepted as possible.

Evolution of the consequences

Turning from the natural history of the *syndrome* to the unfolding of the history of accompanying *disabilities*, one is dealing with very different matters. To use the term 'natural history' with its medical implications and connotations of pathological process is legitimate when discussing a psychobiological syndrome. But the accumulation of alcohol-related disabilities involves the social sphere and all manner of interactive processes, as well as the drinker's socio-economic position and his personality, and all these to such an extent that variation makes nonsense of any generalizations based on the medical idea of 'pathological process'. At one extreme, the bank manager with this disorder may remain largely socially integrated until, at the age of fifty-five, his physical health gives way. His wife may have been irritated by his habit of falling asleep after dinner and found him dull company, his colleagues may have found him a little irritable and slow on the job, but as dependence has advanced social disintegration has certainly not advanced at the same pace. In contrast, an unskilled labourer who is single, a bit of a drifter, impulsive, and anxious, with only tenuous adjustment at the best of times, may develop alcohol dependence in his early thirties, and may then find that, very much in parallel, he is losing employment, is being arrested for public intoxication, is having short periods in prison, is moving towards the forgiving friendship of the bottle-gang in the park at first as a peripheral member, and then heading rapidly towards Skid Row and total degradation – and with morning shakes relieved by a swig of surgical spirits. In many different ways, the way in which society, and the individual's close associates, deal with the drinker will affect the development of consequences. Getting sacked, divorced, or arrested will cut the strands of the network of social supports and may lead to increased dependence which, in turn, may cause further social disapproval and isolation.

The implications of the alcohol dependence syndrome

What then are the immediate implications of alcohol being a drug with dependence-producing properties? It may be best to look at this under three different headings: the implications for the individual dependent drinker; those for his family; and those for society at large.

For the individual the implications are that he is handling a substance which is dangerous not only in direct terms of the disabilities it may inflict (Chapter 5), but dangerous also because he finds himself drinking more heavily than he had ever originally intended, and is not able to pull back easily at all. Once a person has become severely dependent he generally has little choice between continuing to drink destructively or stopping drinking altogether. He needs to come to terms with the fact that he has developed an unpleasant and destructive condition, and unless he stops drinking he is likely either dramatically to wreck himself, or slowly and undramatically to ruin his health and happiness. To put matters thus may seem too highly coloured, but the misery for the individual which can often result from alcohol dependence needs to be very clearly realized.

Any person who drinks should be aware that he is using a drug which can induce dependence, and all he need do to contract this condition is to drink for long enough in sufficiently large quantities. No one has a guaranteed immunity. What constitutes the threshold of danger is on present knowledge impossible to state with exactness, but an informed guess might be that anyone who makes a habit of drinking the equivalent of half a bottle of spirits or eight pints of beer daily is putting himself at very considerable risk of acquiring dependence, and this statement should not be taken as meaning that lower levels are necessarily safe. Such estimates are rough and ready, and there are individual variations in what constitutes the danger zone for dependence risk. Those responsible for health education have traditionally been shy of giving any figures at all, for fear that a statement on danger levels could be taken by some individuals as an invitation to drink to the very edge of any stated limits. The levels of drink which may harm health are lower than those which induce dependence, and the main question of what constitutes 'safe drinking' is discussed later (pp. 140–41).

The implications for that person's family are that unless they understand what they are dealing with, they will be apt to use the wrong tactics. The analogy might be with the mistake that would result if a man's wife tried to jolly him out of his 'indigestion', when he was in fact beginning to experience symptoms of a duodenal ulcer. Drinking, where the problem has progressed to a stage of well-established alcohol dependence, is not going to be brought back under control by any amount of cajolery, scolding, or temporary striking of bargains.

As for the implications for society, there must be a realization that we live in a country in which the dependence syndrome is going to be one of the general facts of life. We have to acknowledge that there will be many people in our drinking society who are using alcohol in a way that is excessive, but which, because of the very nature of dependence, is not going to be brought back under control by ordinary disapprobations or punishments. Taking an alcohol-dependent person off one's list of friends will not necessarily make him drink more reasonably, and neither in all probability will sacking him, or putting him in prison. It is this diminished responsiveness to ordinary social remedies that so often frustrates society's well-meaning efforts to deal with a condition by using methods which are largely inappropriate to the nature of that condition, and which may if anything make matters worse. The implications of alcohol being a drug of dependence have therefore to be considered not just by the families of those people, not just by the professionals responsible for treatment and the government departments responsible for organizing treatment, but by everyone. The alcohol-dependent person may be our employer or employee, our burglar, our policeman, or our judge, our patient or our doctor, our father or our daughter, or ourselves.

Dependence and the ideas of sin and disease

In the light of what has been discussed in this chapter about the nature and significance of the dependence syndrome, this is the point again to take up the questions of 'models of understanding' (pp. 21–2).

The sin model

What are the social profits and losses which follow from the sin or self-indulgence types of formulation? The immediate profit for society is that there is someone other than society to blame: we can hardly ourselves be expected to take blame or responsibility for people who of their own unimpaired and sinful volition drink in a manner that causes them to suffer. If they fall down in the street they should be fined, and if they cannot pay the fine they should go to prison. The majority of the 100,000 arrests a year for public drunkenness are of people who are not casual roisterers, but men or women severely dependent on alcohol. The sin model of excessive drinking, though not one on which any Minister of State would care publicly to take his stand, thus still dictates aspects of the way things are officially handled. It also influences or wholly dictates the dealings of many ordinary citizens with the excessive drinker with whom they come in contact: the person they sack, the woman who is no longer asked to dinner, the person who in every sense we pass by on the other side of the street.

A harshness in public attitudes towards the victim might also be thought to deter some people from drinking in such a manner as to contract the dependence syndrome, but this may not in fact be effective. Society can happily condemn the advanced case of alcohol dependence while in no way disapproving the type of drinking that leads to that condition. In terms even of society's self-interests the model soon ceases to be very satisfactory. We find that we are passing by the same man many times, that there seem to be rather a lot of such people, that their behaviour is not only unsightly but costly, and that punitive attitudes or legally inflicted punishments do little to deter this behaviour. Punishing the heavily dependent person seems pragmatically as ineffective as whipping the mentally ill or imprisoning the bankrupt. The sin model is simply not a good basis for effective policies in society's interests, even disregarding its invitations to inhumanity.

The disease mode

Not surprisingly, therefore, an alternative model has been sought, and the most important contender of recent years has been the *disease concept of alcoholism* – with the word 'alcoholism' used here in a manner synonymous with the alcohol dependence syndrome. The statement that 'alcoholism is a disease' has at times been propagated without asking what is meant by 'disease',

54

or by 'alcoholism'. This model has recently come in for some questioning.

Leaving aside for the moment any questions as to the scientific validity of the disease concept, it is again possible to examine the social profit and loss which comes from looking at the condition in this way. The likely immediate gains are of course evident in the kinder approach which this model should propose in our dealings with the individual – if he is ill, we should take him to a hospital rather than a police cell, we should perhaps give him sick leave rather than sack him, we should think of marital therapy rather than advise immediate divorce, and so on.

There is though a danger in the disease concept if a consequence is that privileged status is then given to the subgroup of excessive drinkers who manifest the dependence syndrome, while those many people who are drinking self-damagingly but who have not developed this syndrome are considered to be undeserving of help and concern. This sharp dichotomy has at times found expression in the distinction between 'the real alcoholic' and 'the drunk'. All that has been said in this chapter about the reality of the dependence syndrome intentionally supports the notion that there is something special about the position of a particular and identifiable subgroup of excessive drinkers. But the person suffering from the syndrome is not an automaton in the grip of an all-controlling and pathological process which totally denies his self-responsibility, while at the same time it must be realized that the man who is drinking excessively at weekends, and who is violent when drunk, may demand sensitive and compassionate understanding as someone who for reasons of personality and circumstance has the greatest difficulty in controlling his impulses.

The model best suited to society's needs

Alcohol problems provide an unusually visible demonstration of the importance of society's ideas as determinants of social transactions. There is the real question as to whether the policeman or the ambulanceman picks up the drunk collapsed in the street.

Which way of looking at things can today be recommended as

best suited to society's needs? What we are looking for here is not the most scientifically correct manner of defining alcohol dependence: the discussion of the psychobiological basis given earlier in this chapter should make it clear that science is at present in no position to rule dogmatically on the nature of the dependence syndrome. But the scientific evidence does strongly suggest that what the alcohol-dependent person has long been telling us about his sense of compulsion, his craving, and his impaired ability to control his drinking probably has a basis in physiological and psychological processes which we are beginning to unravel. The dependent person's relationship with alcohol is not on the same footing as it was in his predependent, heavy-drinking days. He has acquired a serious disorder. Perhaps in these terms it would be best, in our particular society and at the present time, to look on alcohol dependence as a disease, but with the added insistence that society has to take an informed rather than a mechanical view of what is meant by that statement.

It is in accord with an informed notion of illness to see the individual as retaining much responsibility for helping himself. And there is nothing in such a view that denies an awareness of the social and psychological factors in the genesis of the disorder, its perpetuation, or what happens to the ill person. Neither is the individual's self-responsibility denied. Indeed, the view of alcohol dependence which we would invite is not unique: the model is one which should be the theme (with many variations) in understanding much of what we today call disease or illness, composed of biological factors but also of social labels and of concepts of self. If society is able to find a satisfactory way of looking at alcohol dependence, it may in the process have found an appropriate way of looking at much else besides.

5

Alcohol-related
disabilities

In this chapter the different types of damage that can result from excessive drinking will be examined. What we are concerned with here is the great array of minor or major problems, mishaps, or damages, in which drinking can be a causal or contributory factor. The person who sustains these disabilities may or may not be suffering from the dependence syndrome. The aim is to give a broad picture of the types of problem that occur and the frequency of their occurrence, rather than to attempt exhaustive listings.

General considerations

For convenience, matters will be considered under the three headings of social, mental, and physical, but the reality of the individual's experience perhaps more usually involves a clustering of problems and varieties of interaction – because of his drinking his wife leaves him (social disability) and he becomes very unhappy (mental disability), and then drinks even more heavily and damages his liver (physical disability).

What must also be emphasized is that disabilities exist in degrees, and what is particularly needed is an awareness of the minor and less dramatic degrees of damage that alcohol can inflict on any particular aspect of the individual's life. Everyone knows that grossly excessive drinking can lead to the break-up of a marriage: what is not so well within the public's consciousness is the frequency with which drinking may rather undramatically damage a marriage. There are too many silly arguments, and neither partner puts the cause down to drinking. Time in the pub becomes more important than time at home. The home is always just that little bit short of money. Too often it is only ten years later, and when the problem has progressed to the point of marital breakdown, that the couple look back and realize that alcohol has been eroding the happiness of their marriage for a long time.

The question of causality, the precise meaning to be given to 'related' in 'alcohol-related disabilities', needs scrutiny. It is usually false to suggest explanations in terms of single causes: the marriage did not break down simply because of the drinking, but also perhaps because of temperamental differences between two people, because of an interfering mother-in-law, because of poor housing, and so on. These factors may all indeed have contributed to the drinking; and the drinking then makes everything worse, and the process becomes circular. Such a perspective is important for sympathetic understanding of the individual case, and as a basis for understanding the varied types of help which may be needed.

As an illustration, here is an account given by a woman:

'I'd say the first year of our marriage was all right, but then after the baby was born and we were still living with my parents and hadn't got a place of our own, well he'd go off with some of his old friends and you can't blame him. When we got the council flat, that was a bit better, but after our third kid was born I was very depressed and I think that got him down. We had rows, and I'd threaten to go back to my mum. Then he was out of work and that didn't help. I suppose looking back a lot of those rows were when he had been drinking, and the first time he hit me.'

The insufficiency of seeing that family's problems as due solely to alcohol is manifest. The crudeness of that assumption is dangerous. But perhaps the more common danger lies in overlooking the subtly destructive influences of the excessive drinking: without the drinking, that young couple's marriage might have worked out happily, they might have coped more constructively with the very real stresses of their environment, and anger need not have turned to violence.

Given the provenance of this Report, it may seem surprising that the section on social disabilities is longer than the sections either on mental or on physical disabilities. We believe indeed that social disabilities should now receive wide attention. This should not be taken to imply an underrating of the profound seriousness of the many possible adverse effects of heavy drinking on mental and physical health, and those elements of disability will also be examined.

Social disabilities

The idea of social disability implies the failure of the individual to perform adequately in any role expected of him (husband, father, or employee, for instance). A closely linked idea is failure to meet expected obligations – for example, to contribute to the national wealth. The concept can also comprise the notion of any behaviour which positively transgresses social rules – crime, sexual deviation, or simply 'being an alcoholic'. That social disability is highly relativistic needs to be stressed, and the judgements involved are by their nature arbitrary, with society the rule-maker and referee. The rules may be different for men and women, for different age groups, between social classes, and certainly between countries. Happy and undramatically successful social adjustment is always something of a balancing act. One important aspect of the disability may be the way in which society reacts to the person who is manifesting that disability, since this may amplify the handicap – the man who for instance cannot get a job 'because he is an alcoholic'.

Social disability and the family

The impact of excessive drinking on marriage was given in the introduction to this chapter as an example of the graduated nature of alcohol-related disabilities, and the multiplicity of its causes. Divorce is common: a survey of Alcoholics Anonymous showed that drinking had broken up marriages in over 30 per cent of members. As for violence, in one study of 100 battered wives, fifty-two of the victims reported that their partners engaged in frequent heavy drinking. Excessive drinking contributes in an important degree to the work of all manner of social agencies and courts which deal with problems of families and children.

The tangible effects on the excessive drinker's wife of large stresses, the accumulation of small stresses, and the continuing uncertainty of how each day will turn out, are several. Some wives may show for a long period an extraordinary capacity to cope and put on a bold front: they will be smartly dressed, the children will look well cared for, the house will be spick and span, and the neighbours will not know that there is anything amiss. Money problems will be met by the wife going out to work and perhaps undertaking further training.

More often the impact of stresses soon becomes obvious. Friends and neighbours when they see that wife ask her, 'What's wrong?' She is obviously a bit worn and tense. She may well start to shut herself off from social contacts just because she doesn't want to be asked this kind of question, and thus she becomes increasingly isolated. She goes to the doctor about her 'bad nerves' and, if he is not someone to whom she feels she can talk (and a person who has time to listen), her distress will simply be met with the prescription of a tranquillizer. A woman who is under such stress may indeed develop a depressive illness, and when she comes to a psychiatric clinic this can be the first occasion on which her husband's problem comes to notice.

Sometimes the first indication may be when the wife makes a suicidal gesture as a plea for help. A recent study showed that one-third of women admitted to hospital because of a drug overdose had a complaint about their husbands' drinking. The family's problem may also come to notice when the wife turns up at a casualty depurtment with bruises or broken bones. Occasionally she will herself start drinking excessively, perhaps to 'try to teach my husband a lesson'. More rarely a woman will, in desperation, physically assault her drinking husband, and the extreme result has on rare occasion been murder.

To discuss the impact of drinking on marriage without referring to the situation where the wife is the excessive drinker would be incomplete. The disruption that can result in that situation is often marked by a great deal of distress and confusion, and coloured by the general tendency of society to be particularly punitive and moralistic towards the woman with a drinking problem. A husband may be ashamed and angry that his wife is bringing disgrace on the family. A woman may see her drunken husband as frightening, while a husband seems often to react to a drunken wife with a revulsion that is linked to basic feelings about betrayal of the goodness and purity of womanhood. Anger may turn to violence and, for economic reasons, it is usually easier for a man to leave a drinking wife than the other way round.

The disabilities which affect the children of a family in which there is a drinking problem can be devastating. The child may have to endure the perpetual rowing between his parents or be witness to scenes of physical violence. The drunken parent may repeatedly pick on one particular child in the family as a target for nagging and demeaning verbal attack, or actual violence.

'You could always tell when he'd been drinking. He'd pick on John, our second son, he's just twelve years old now. Say he was no good, wasn't a real boy. My husband was an athlete you see, and John is on the slight side, a bit weedy, wears glasses. He'd be at him again as soon as he got into the house. Go up close and shout at him. The boy would go so terrified he wouldn't be able to speak and then his father would shout at him for an answer.'

It is not only the positive traumas that can damage the child's health and emotional growth, but the negative effect of the lack of a good relationship and of a consistent model.

The immediate consequence may be that the child develops overt neurotic symptoms, or shows behaviour disorders, or engages in delinquency. An adverse impact on school work is common. In adolescence escape may be found by spending little time in the home to which a son is ashamed to invite his friends, and finding a set of friends outside with whom he can identify – he may drift to a peer group which is itself in some way disturbed (a group for instance in which a lot of drinking or drug taking goes on). The impact can be as great on a girl as a boy, and the psychological damage done to a girl who is torn between love and hatred for a drunken and unpredictable father can be devastating. Indeed, in many instances the emotional harm done in childhood, whether to son or daughter, will result in disabilities which continue into that child's adult life.

Drinking problems and employment

Excessive drinking can result in sacking, repeated sacking, and then virtual unemployability. It often means a slide into less skilled and responsible work. In a study of Alcoholics Anonymous to which reference has already been made, 63 per cent of the men had at some time been sacked because of their drinking. An earlier study showed that, in a predominantly middle-class group of alcoholic patients attending Warlingham Park Hospital, 52 per cent had been sacked for drinking. In a survey of people attending counselling centres affiliated to the National Council on Alcoholism, 45 per cent were currently sick or unemployed. Of the total, 47 per cent said that their present or most recent job represented a demotion in wage terms. Forty-three per cent believed that their drinking had caused or contributed to an accident at work.

However, the impact of excessive drinking on employment must be seen not only in terms of sackings and long spells out of work, but also in more subtle processes. A man is still at work, but is not working efficiently, is getting in someone else's way, or leaving someone else to do the job for him. He may not be sacked, but is promoted sideways, or retired with a costly golden handshake. Drink-related problems are likely to be experienced at every level in industry and commerce, and are as often to be found in the board room as on the shop floor.

Drinking and crime

The relationship between drinking and crime emphasizes the need to think about causal systems rather than single causes. A criminal offence is seldom committed for one isolated and simple reason – for instance, a woman steals from a shop when she is drinking, but she is also depressed and has become impulsive or wants to be caught and given help. Because she is obviously shabby and drunk and the shop employs a store detective, she is caught. To say that drinking 'caused this crime' would be an oversimplification.

The connections between crime and drinking appear to be of several types. First there is the fact that being drunk and incapable in a public place, or drunk and disorderly, constitute offences. Strictly speaking it is not the intoxication itself which is the offence, but the immediate consequences of the intoxication. The discussion on Skid Row in the next section of this chapter should make it clear that, although a man is arrested on a drinking charge, drinking may be only one facet of the problem. Drunken driving will also be given separate consideration under a later heading.

The bulk of alcohol-related crime is comprised of petty offences committed by people who are caught up in a way of life characterized by social instability – people who are unskilled, who do not stay for long in one job, who are homeless and often itinerant between cities, and who are in many ways socially and personally handicapped. The man who is prone to break society's rules in small ways is even more likely to commit some foolish and not very profitable theft when drunk, to throw a stone through a window, to beg, to assault a policeman, or to urinate on a doorstep. If he does this sort of thing often enough and cannot pay the fine, he may well find himself in prison. Such a crime is often described as petty or minor, but it all contributes to a process which can be profoundly disruptive to an individual's life adjustment. He is dragged further into an entanglement from which he cannot escape, and repeated short-term imprisonment only exacerbates his predicament. He may as an individual be a very unimportant 'criminal', but the sum total of such people makes a major contribution to the work load of the courts and the population of the prisons. The story of the drinking problem is seldom seen as worth pleading. Different studies of prisoners in England and Scotland have suggested that half to two-thirds of the men had a serious drinking problem and about 15 per cent of women prisoners, and most of these were petty recidivists.

There is also an association between drinking and some more specific and serious types of offence. There can be no doubt that excessive drinking quite often lies behind the story of the accountant who is suddenly discovered to have defrauded his firm of thousands of pounds or the solicitor who has betrayed his client's trust, or (much more often and on the less grand scale) of the storeman who has been selling off his firm's goods. Drinking costs money, and that solicitor may not only have been spending £2,000 each year directly on alcohol, but his drinking may in addition have led him into a life style where profligate spending is the order of the day. Excessive drinking thus certainly makes its contribution to 'white-collar crime', as well as to the problems of Skid Row.

Drinking also seems to be related quite frequently to the acting out of sexual fantasies which are otherwise kept under control. The sexual assault on a child, the previously respectable citizen picked up for soliciting in a public lavatory, the sadistic rape, are all types of offence where intoxication is often an important contributory cause to behaviour which would be entirely out of keeping with the person's character, and which may leave him aghast when he sobers up and realizes what he has done.

Another connection is that between alcohol and crimes of violence. The incident may be no more than the punch-up on the pavement outside the pub at closing time when a drunken man becomes cantankerous, but with intoxication there is always the possibility of sudden extreme loss of impulse-control, and of violence going beyond anything originally intended. A marital argument may, for instance, suddenly become brutally serious, and a knife is used. Studies of the relationship between intoxication and murder have generally shown that in about half the cases the murderer is intoxicated at the time of the killing (and murder is, of course, very largely a family crime). There is further evidence to suggest that the victim, too, may often have been drinking at the time of the murder.

Putting together what is known of the considerable involvement of excessive drinking in the petty recidivism that crowds our prisons, the direct involvement of drinking in the public drunkenness offence and in drunken driving, the role of drinking in financial offences, its involvement in sexual offences, and its contribution to crimes of violence, it becomes evident that we have here another major reason for society to be concerned about drinking. Even with cautious regard for the need to work with an idea of 'cause' which is subtle and complex rather than single-factor, it is clear that, in any debate about crime prevention, in help for offenders, or in the costing of the national bill for crime and correction, excessive drinking must be a major and recurrent theme.

But even so, to put this problem under the general heading of 'alcohol-related disabilities' might at first seem strange. Given that society foots a considerable bill, that the person at the receiving end of petty crime suffers minor loss or inconvenience, or that the occasional victim of the major alcohol-related offence is grossly harmed, it may seem too compassionate to designate the person who *commits* these offences as suffering from a disability. The term is however being used advisedly, for the person who commits such crimes is often involved in a process which is as damaging to himself as to society:

> 'It was stupid. I just went up the front steps, into the hall-way, took an alarm clock, and then I was so drunk I fell down the steps. That's what they tell me, but I don't remember anything about it. That's always what happens when I go on the drink – I go and nick something absolutely stupid, in broad daylight. The magistrate gave me a chance last time, but you can't blame him, he's fed up now.'

There is no one case which can illustrate the whole range of alcohol-related crimes. There are certainly instances where the offender appears primarily to be a career criminal, and he has developed a drinking problem rather late in the course of that career. Drink has been employed to provide Dutch courage for quite intentional crime, and one may sometimes suspect that drinking is being used as an excuse for behaviour that was soberly premeditated.

But the more closely one looks at the man who steals the alarm clock, the accountant who embezzles, the man who knifes his wife in a drunken quarrel, the more does one see the common elements of behaviour that would have been unlikely to have occurred without drinking, behaviour characterized by lack of impulse control or so out of character as to suggest marked impairment of personality, which brings that individual little or nothing in the way of real gain or satisfaction, and which has as its largest result a disability that is the erosion or destruction of that person's place in society.

Skid Row and the chronic drunkenness offender

In most large British cities the sight of a couple of ragged men sitting together in a doorway, sharing the contents of a bottle, is not unfamiliar. There may be particular street corners or parks where such men are especially likely to congregate, or they may make the main-line railway station their haunt. Occasionally there is a woman in the group, but the problem exists primarily among males. There are over 10,000 people in this country who belong to the drifting world of what is often termed 'Skid Row'.

In American cities, 'Skid Row' has been used to describe well-known and circumscribed city areas such as the Bowery in New York. The phrase catches the image of broken-down housing, an area of rooming houses and cheap hotels, streets where the doorways will be littered with empty bottles, and a population of destitutes. Many of these people will be chronically heavy drinkers, but such an area gives a home to every sort of social casualty. A close acquaintance with big cities in the UK reveals a world which in its social meaning is very similar to America's Skid Row, but instead of being concentrated and highly visible, it is diffuse, and easily overlooked.

What in this country is the meaning of the Skid Row way of life? So far as most people are aware of this problem, it seems sad, unsightly, vaguely offensive, and somehow very old-fashioned that there should still be drunken vagrants on our streets. The ordinary citizen may give a few pennies 'for a cup of tea', but how the man who begs from us came to this state, and who he is – such questions tend to remain unasked as we hurry by.

Much information has been gathered recently on the nature of this problem. The destitute man is not necessarily a heavy drinker – he may be eccentric, a schizophrenic drifting without support, someone whose multiple handicaps have somehow dragged him down. Drinking, however, makes a substantial contribution. A study of men resident on a particular census night at the Camberwell Reception Centre in London showed that 49 per cent of that population admitted to drinking problems. The usual picture of Skid Row alcoholism may best be interpreted as that of alcohol dependence shaped by the particular vulnerability of the man who starts with few social supports, and whose drinking then knocks away those minimal supports he did possess.

The Skid Row man is often an immigrant to the city (a survey in London showed that, among a group of fifty-one Skid Row drinkers, 37 per cent were Irish and 27 per cent were Scottish), and he is perhaps using the anonymity of that city as some sort of retreat or hiding place. He often comes from a home which has been handicapping, and 58 per cent of men in the London Skid Row study had experienced parental separation in childhood. From home he easily moves to drifting and rootlessness. He has probably never been married, and has never had any job skill. The drinking history intertwines with all the other social handicaps. He probably starts to drink regularly as soon as he leaves home. By the time he is thirty he has contracted marked alcohol dependence. In his early thirties an alcohol-related offence takes him for the first time to prison. By his late thirties he is 'on Skid Row' – chronically drunk, repeatedly arrested, in and out of prison for short sentences, sleeping in derelict houses or cheap hostels, totally isolated from friends or family. He is in a situation from which it is exceedingly difficult to find any way back. He drinks cheap wine, cider, or surgical spirits. Life expectancy is greatly shortened.

Skid Row speaks of painful and degrading human problems in their own right. Skid Row also exemplifies certain generally important truths. It provides an instance of society's inability to live with some painful realities other than by strategies of denial and avoidance. Skid Row has always been someone else's problem. It shows our ability to get caught up in absurd and unproductive responses – the man who is arrested 100 times for public drunkenness will inevitably be dealt with in exactly the same way for the one-hundred-and-first offence. In a study conducted some years ago in London, 150 men were interviewed who appeared before two courts on drunkenness offences. For 25 per cent of these men it was their second drunkenness arrest within the space of one month, and 50 per cent of the total had been arrested at least once before during the previous year; 10 per cent had been arrested more than ten times during the previous year. About 50 per cent showed evidence of the fully developed alcohol dependence syndrome, and a further 25 per cent, though not manifesting this syndrome, nonetheless revealed a serious drinking problem. They showed an extraordinary degree of social isolation: almost 60 per cent were homeless, over half had not had contact with parents or siblings for over a year, and 40 per cent were unemployed at the time of interview. More than half came originally from Scotland or Ireland. The problems of the chronic drunkenness offence and of Skid Row largely overlap.

Table 2 gives figures for annual convictions for public drunkenness over recent decades. There was a fall during the last war, and then, again, a rise. Greater national prosperity and the Welfare State have manifestly failed to diminish (let alone eliminate) a legacy of the nineteenth century.

Drunken driving

The Report of the recent government committee on drinking and driving (the Blennerhassett Committee – see p. 18) gives an estimate of the total annual cost to this country of road accidents in which alcohol is involved. The estimate amounts to an astonish-

Table 2 Findings of guilt for offences of drunkenness proved in England and Wales 1950–77

Year	Numbers of offences	Number per 10,000 popuiation aged 15 years and over (1950–68) or 14 years and over (1969 forward)
1950	47,717	14·0
1951	53,676	15·8
1952	53,888	15·8
1953	53,574	15·7
1954	53,277	15·5
1955	54,210	15·8
1956	60,182	17·4
1957	67,002	19·3
1958	65,058	18·7
1959	65,187	18·6
1960	68,109	19·3
1961	74,694	21·0
1962	83,992	23·3
1963	83,007	22·8
1964	76,842	21·0
1965	72,980	19·8
1966	70,499	19·0
1967	75,544	20·3
1968	79,070	21·2
1969	80,502	21·2
1970	82,374	21·6
1971	86,735	22·9
1972	90,198	23·7
1973	99,274	25·9
1974	103,203	26·8
1975	104,452	27·0
1976	108,698	28·0
1977	108,871	27·9

Source: Annual Home Office Reports and *Offences of Drunkenness, 1970* (London: HMSO.)

ing £100 million per year – a figure which must include damage to vehicles (and insurance claims), medical treatment of casualties, sickness benefits, police and court work, and so on. And these are only the economic costs of drinking and driving. To audit the cost in terms of suffering and distress is more difficult. Detailed investigations of accidents by the Transport and Road Research Laboratory showed that in 1974 one in three (about 900) drivers killed in road accidents had blood alcohol levels above the statutory limit; between 10 pm and 4 am on Monday to Friday the proportion of driver fatalities with blood alcohol over the legal limit rose to 51 per cent, and on Saturday nights to 71 per cent. In a survey of 2,000 road accidents, a drinking driver was involved in 25 per cent, and his condition deemed to be a major factor in 9 per cent. Drinking significantly contributes to accidents of all degrees of severity, and perhaps particularly to the more serious accidents. Another obvious aspect of social cost is the tally of 63,000 convictions for drunken driving in one year (1976), with costs to the police and to the court, and many aspects of cost to the individual who almost invariably has his licence suspended.

As with alcohol and crime in general, the question which must immediately come to mind is whether we are sliding too easily towards an assumption of cause, when only statistical association is being demonstrated. This query will not only be raised, very properly, by the dispassionate critic who has a wary eye for this kind of logical error, but also by the drinker who wants to persuade himself that personally his drinking only improves his driving. A mass of scientific evidence does however speak to the causal nature of the demonstrated relationship, and this is now a matter on which it is right to take a position unqualified by reservations.

The evidence comes partly from laboratory tests, which show the well-known impact of alcohol on reaction time. Such laboratory findings are at considerable remove from the realities of the drive home on Saturday night, but it cannot be doubted that the physiological fact of impaired reaction time will have its practical effect when, after his evening in the pub, the driver suddenly has to make some fairly normal but split-second driving decision on which safety depends. A number of experiments on driving after drink, conducted with volunteers, have shown the manner in which judgement and skill are actually affected – the classic experiment with the volunteer bus drivers has already been mentioned (p. 33).

But the most conclusive evidence comes from a survey conducted by the police department in Grand Rapids, Michigan, which obtained vital control information. For every person who had an accident the blood alcohol level was obtained, and then control information was obtained by stopping motorists at the same accident points, and obtaining their blood alcohol levels. This sort of data allows rejection of the argument that at that time of night a high percentage of all drivers will have been drinking. The Grand Rapids survey was able to give an estimate of the risk of being involved in an accident as a function of increased blood alcohol level, compared to sober drivers in the control group. At 80 mg % alcohol (the British legal limit), the accident risk shows an increase approaching twice the sober risk level, by 150 mg % the risk was ten times the normal, and by 200 mg % the risk of accident was twenty times the normal level.

To argue the causal relationship between drinking and driving accidents is in no way to deny the multiple causes of most accidents, but only to insist that drinking frequently makes a major contribution to the mishap. The age and the motoring experience of the driver are certainly also important, as are his personality and his alertness or fatigue. The road surface, lighting, and general driving conditions will bear on the likelihood of accident, as will the mechanical efficiency of the car, the behaviour of other drivers, and the behaviour of pedestrians. But the addition to a total situation of the driver's inebriety may often crucially tip the balance between safety and danger.

In 1967 the *Road Traffic Act* led to the introduction of the breathalyzer, and fixed the permitted statutory level of 80 mg %. Parliament rejected the notion of random breath testing. The Act was preceded by an intensive publicity campaign. There is much evidence that the combination of new legislation, energetic enforcement, and public education produced immediate and dramatic effect. It has been calculated that about 5,000 lives have been saved, and 200,000 casualties. Road casualties fell immediately by 11 per cent and deaths by 15 per cent. But over the ensuing years the effects of these measures were gradually eroded – the publicity was not sustained, the public seemed to forget the message, and various loopholes in the law hampered the task of enforcement. *Figure 1* gives data on drunken driving

Figure 1   *Drinking and driving prosecutions (England and Wales)*

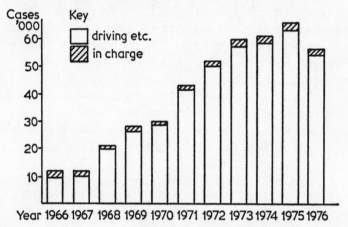

Year 1966 1967 1968 1969 1970 1971 1972 1973 1974 1975 1976

Source: Adapted from a figure in the *Report of the Departmental Committee on Drinking and Driving* (1976) (Blennerhassett Committee) with additional information obtained by personal communication with the DHSS.

convictions from 1966 to 1976. The general up-swing in alcohol consumption (and in the number of licensed vehicles) will also have tended to force the drunk-driving casualty figures up again. No-one can say how bad things would have been in the absence of this legislation, but certainly by 1974 the situation was again causing such official concern that a departmental committee was appointed.

This committee reported in 1976, and made a variety of technical recommendations which, if introduced, would enable tighter enforcement. Technical advances in breath testing equipment mean, for instance, that it is now possible for breath testing at the roadside followed by a breath test in the police station to be recommended as sufficient evidence, rather than incurring the delays and procedural uncertainties inherent in getting the police surgeon to conduct the additional statutory blood test. The burden of the committee's report was not that there should be more draconian punishment (or a lower statutory blood level), but that there should be movement towards a law that would allow a manifestly greater likelihood of apprehending and successfully prosecuting the offender. The notion of 'random breath testing' is emotionally charged because of the fear of possible needless harrassment, but the committee recommended more police discretion concerning the circumstances in which a driver may be asked to take a test. Legislation is now awaited.

What percentage of people arrested for drunken driving are drinkers who generally drink in a rather temperate manner, as compared to the proportion contributed by drinkers whose habits are more excessive or who are alcohol dependent? In this country there appears to be no solid evidence on this point. Half of the first offenders are, however, found to have a blood alcohol level of over 150 mg %, which represents a level probably not commonly reached by the light or infrequent drinker. Among second offenders, two-thirds exceed this level. The indications suggest, therefore, that many of these arrests are of heavy drinkers.

Economic costs of alcohol-related problems

The adverse effects of alcohol misuse impose a significant economic burden on society. Reference has already been made to the cost of drunken driving (see *Drunken driving* above). It would never be possible to place a reliable economic value on adverse effects such as broken homes and disturbed children, and because of insufficient data or still-inadequate methodology it is not yet possible to arrive at the cost of certain effects in which the economic component is more obvious, such as loss of production in industry. However, estimates were developed of the annual costs of alcohol misuse in the United States in 1971. The cost assigned to lost industrial production was $9·35 billion. The costs of medical services were estimated at $8·29 billion, traffic accidents at $6·44 billion, the bill to the criminal justice system at

$0·51 billion dollars, and alcohol-related programmes and research cost $0·64 billion. The grand annual total was $25·37 billion. America has a population four times greater than that of Britain, and in proportion to population a higher alcoholism rate.

But if this country had the data to carry out a similar audit, it cannot be doubted that the total bill here too would be staggering.

Mental disabilities

Alcohol and mood

Alcohol relieves unpleasant mental feelings, and this will be discussed later in relation to the question of why people drink. But no drug taken to relieve deep-seated feelings of unease with life, self-doubt, or chronic tension will put those feelings right except very transiently. Because alcohol is a drug to which tolerance develops, the likelihood is that alcohol will gradually be needed in larger and larger quantities, for the development of tolerance means that more of a drug is required to produce the same effects as before. Not only does drinking then begin to fail in its original purpose of relieving psychological distress and creating a happier mood, but it begins to make matters worse. Heavy drinking itself begins to produce 'bad nerves', and the person concerned easily misinterprets this as a condition which requires further drink to put it right. Alcohol in large and continued quantities can itself produce a very depressing effect on mood, and the person becomes prey to all sorts of doubts, miseries, suspicions, and general gloom. He may also develop acute fear of particular situations. This may be exacerbated by failing health, and the evident and undeniable accumulation of social problems which are legitimate causes for worry.

Heavy drinking thus easily leads to a state of mental distress which is not only misinterpreted by the subject himself, but which a doctor is apt to diagnose simply as 'depression' or 'anxiety' if the drinking story is missed. Treatment with anti-depressants or tranquillizers will usually be ineffective, and can make matters worse. Since minor tranquillizers are themselves central

74

nervous system depressants, they are likely to compound the effects of alcohol and, more seriously, delay the discovery of the correct diagnosis.

This slow development of mental distress contributes to the appallingly high rate of suicide associated with alcoholism, although this is also a section of the population at particular risk because of underlying psychological problems which may be present. Much greater awareness of the possible involvement of alcohol in suicide and attempted suicide is needed. A report from the Regional Poisoning Treatment Centre in Edinburgh showed that in 1975 45 per cent of all male first admissions had a drinking problem (with one-third of that proportion showing signs of the alcohol dependence syndrome). During the same year 14 per cent of female first admissions to the Poisoning Centre were diagnosed as having a drinking problem.

It should be realized that, as self-prescribed treatment for real psychological problems, alcohol is a thoroughly dangerous medicine. Anyone who thinks he is drinking because of his 'nerves' must also ask whether his 'nerves' are troubled because of his drinking. To the medical profession it should be clear that 'bad nerves' or 'depression' should never be treated until enquiry has been made into the patient's drinking.

Alcohol and its influence on personality

As with its effect on mood, it has to be admitted that the personality troubles which come from heavy drinking stem from an over-use of alcohol for purposes which are widely accepted. In a subtle way, one of the prime accepted uses of alcohol is to drink so that we will be rather different people. We will not only feel differently ourselves after a few drinks, but will act differently and be perceived differently by others. Drinking to harmonize interaction between people is likely to be at its maximum if both people are drinking rather than only one.

The hoped-for cosmetic effect of drinking on personality is that it should make us into jollier people, more confident, more extroverted, less guarded, more readily able to laugh, and generally better able to interact with other people. Our emotions are more readily available. We ourselves will feel more amusing, more powerful and important, and perhaps more sexual.

The disadvantage may be that some of the effects of even moderate drinking on personality are not so attractive. Some people simply become bores. They are loquacious, and only want to talk about themselves. They may become boastful and silly. The supposed warmth of the interpersonal reactions can be a charade. All this may be irritating and distasteful to the member of the party who is more sober than the others, but is generally more likely to be dreary than harmful. It is when such behaviour is regularly repeated, and someone who does not much like it has frequently to put up with it, that harm is done. This is what so often happens when one partner in a marriage is steadily or intermittently drinking heavily – the same issue has been discussed in a preceding section (p. 60). A husband may be stupidly embarrassing at parties or in the pub. The wife is fed up with his boastfulness, silly stories, and pseudosexuality. He is perhaps tending towards the company of drinking friends who can enjoy the same superficialities. If she complains, there is a row, he claims to be hurt and sulks, and he may become abusive. The deterioration of behaviour towards friends, colleagues, employers, and neighbours gradually wears out the heavy drinker's credit and reputation.

As the severity of a drinking problem and its chronicity advance, a person's previous personality may appear to be greatly altered for the worse, and hence the notion of 'personality deterioration'. When matters become as seemingly fixed as this, one is talking about the more serious end of the spectrum. Friends will report that 'you simply can't believe anything he says'. This is not an inevitable consequence even of chronic very heavy drinking, but in some degree it is not an uncommon picture. The drinker is then often labelled as suffering from severe personality disorder or psychopathy. The development of this sort of pattern is as much due to the chronically fraught and chaotic situation in which a person finds himself, as to the toxic effects of alcohol. He repeatedly breaks his word because, when drinking is an imperative priority over all other considerations, he is in no position to keep his word.

A frequent symptom of heavy drinking is a short-term *amnesia* or 'memory blackout'. In the morning the drinker cannot remember the events of the evening before, although during that evening he was fully conscious and joining in a passionate argument. This has sometimes been described as a certain sign of 'alcoholism', but is in fact a symptom which may have been experienced by 15 per cent to 20 per cent of men who drink. It is certainly a serious warning sign. With increasingly serious drinking, amnesias may begin to occur with great frequency, and even up to a few days of experience may be completely 'blacked out'. These happenings can be extremely frightening and perplexing for the person concerned. Recent research has been focussing on the brain mechanisms that are involved.

The mental complication of excessive drinking which is popularly most widely known is *delirium tremens* or 'the horrors'. The classical picture is easily recognized. The patient is obviously physically ill, agitated, shaking, confused, and talking about his visions and voices. The picture is however not always so clear-cut, and can be mistaken for the delirium of pneumonia or the confusion of a post-operative state. DTs are likely to develop within a few days of alcohol withdrawal or a reduction in alcohol intake, while *withdrawal fits* may occur after about twenty-four hours of abstinence. Although full understanding of the underlying biochemical upsets in delirium tremens is still incomplete, this illness is to a large extent to be understood as an extreme manifestation of the withdrawal syndrome in someone who is highly dependent.

A severe form of alcohol-related mental illness which is not popularly so well known is *alcoholic hallucinosis*: the patient goes about his business and is not physically ill, but he is hearing voices, and the picture can look very like paranoid schizophrenia. A third condition which must be put in the list of major disorders is *alcoholic dementia* – a disorder which will receive further note in the section on physical disorders (p. 82).

Loss of sexual interest, or sexual *impotence*, can occur as a result of chronic heavy alcohol use. Heavy drinking is also said to

77

be associated with the development of abnormal jealousy and, as has been mentioned in discussing alcohol-related crime, the person who is drinking heavily may act out otherwise controlled or subconscious sexual problems. *Gambling* and heavy drinking often go together, sometimes with each seeming to exacerbate the other, or at times one problem substituting for the other.

Heavy alcohol use and *misuse of other drugs* are also not infrequently linked. The drinker feels his nerves are bad and manages to obtain prescriptions for a mass of tranquillizers and sleeping tablets which he then takes in addition to his alcohol, and he develops a serious and additional habit. The nurse, doctor, or pharmacist who has a drinking problem is likely, for obvious reasons of availability, to abuse drugs concurrently. The problem should largely be seen as that of the combined misuse of alcohol and prescribed drugs (sometimes with a disastrous combined overdose), but at times a troubled young person who takes illegal drugs may take them jointly with alcohol. Sometimes the story is of an adolescent who develops a drinking problem a few years after leaving school, starts to use amphetamines and cannabis, in the next phase becomes a narcotic addict, and who then in his late twenties gives up drugs only to encounter problems with drinking once again. Those who are concerned with the rehabilitation of young drug users are today well aware of the danger that an apparent recovery will be destroyed by the development of heavy drinking. The heavy drinker is frequently also a confirmed tobacco smoker.

Physical disabilities

Alcohol can adversely affect physical health in several ways. The person who is drinking too much may, for instance, neglect his diet, and consequently suffer from nutritional deficiencies. Alcohol can have a direct toxic effect on certain body tissues, and this may contribute to liver damage. The person who is intoxicated may injure himself (or others). The general neglect of health and the lowering of the body's resistance can lead to an increased susceptibility to intercurrent infections. Often more than one process operates at the same time. What has to be conveyed is an

78

awareness of the fact that excessive drinking can, in one way or another, damage nearly every organ and system of the body.

Liver damage

Almost everyone is aware that excessive drinking can sometimes result in cirrhosis of the liver. This is an extremely serious and unpleasant condition, with a high expectation of death within a few years if the person then continues to drink. Both length of drinking history and level of drinking bear on the risk of liver damage – in effect, the concern has to be with 'lifetime' intake. There is some dispute as to what constitutes the safe level of alcohol intake, but solid evidence indicates that if someone drinks regularly the equivalent of between five and ten pints of beer or more each day, he increases his risk of contracting cirrhosis. Such levels are below those usually associated with alcohol dependence, but they carry a degree of threat to physical health which has only recently been substantiated. This is one instance of the type of information which is forcing an awareness that concern can no longer be focussed only on extremes of consumption. Certainly, when drinking is extreme and has averaged above ten pints of beer a day for over fifteen years, the individual runs a grave risk of liver damage. Some research reports have suggested that as many as 80 per cent of drinkers in that sort of consumption bracket will damage their livers.

The important message for the patient with alcohol-induced liver disease is that, if he goes on drinking, his liver condition will further deteriorate, with cirrhosis meaning an extremely unpleasant form of invalidism and a much curtailed life expectancy. Emphasis must also be placed on the fact that, if the patient stops drinking, the liver disease will often cease to progress. There are few circumstances in which abstinence can be so life saving. Drinking is by no means the only possible cause of cirrhosis, but over recent years alcoholic cirrhosis has in this country gradually come to make a much larger contribution to the total cirrhosis deathrate than was previously the case: in two studies conducted in Birmingham, the proportion of alcoholic cirrhosis rose from 33 per cent to 51 per cent of total cirrhosis cases, between

1959–64 and 1964–9. A recent study in South London showed alcoholic cirrhotics accounting for 65 per cent of the total cirrhotics. National figures on cirrhosis deaths for the years 1950 to 1976 are given in *Table 3*.

Other forms of liver damage besides cirrhosis can also develop. Inflammation and enlargement due to fatty infiltration are milder problems, which may later lead to cirrhosis. On rare occasions a bout of heavy drinking can cause sudden and devastating inflammation of the liver, and death. Patients with alcoholic cirrhosis may develop a cancer of the liver as an added complication. Deaths from cirrhosis of the liver have been steadily increasing for the past thirty years.

Stomach ulcers and duodenal ulcers

More than 20 per cent of patients with established histories of 'alcoholism' are likely to have developed peptic ulcers. The patient who comes into a hospital as an emergency case with a perforation of his ulcer or bleeding acutely from the stomach is at a disadvantage if he is in a poor general state of health as a result of his drinking, especially if he develops delirium tremens as a consequence of sudden alcohol withdrawal. The exact level of alcohol intake which carries a risk of ulceration is unclear, but most doctors would probably advise a patient with symptoms of peptic ulcer either to moderate or to stop his drinking. Ulcers provide a good example of the need for greater awareness, in general hospitals and general medicine, of the fact that an alcohol problem may not infrequently be hidden behind a common medical disorder. It is all too easy, when a patient has gastritis or an ulcer, to treat this condition and overlook the drinking. The result is a missed opportunity for detection and help. Sadly, it is not unknown for a patient to have an operation, or a couple of operations, for stomach ulcers, without the drinking history being properly elicited. Cirrhosis seems to be in every doctor's mind as a classical consequence of heavy drinking, but not the much more common problem of peptic ulcer.

Table 3 Cirrhosis deaths recorded as alcoholic or other cause, England and Wales

Year	Total deaths due to cirrhosis	Death rates per million all persons
1950	1,016	23
1951	1,117	25
1952	1,124	26
1953	1,155	26
1954	1,168	26
1955	1,159	26
1956	1,153	26
1957	1,206	27
1958	1,146	26
1959	1,203	27
1960	1,272	28
1961	1,370	30
1962	1,302	28
1963	1,325	28
1964	1,309	28
1965	1,384	29
1966	1,366	29
1967	1,350	28
1968	1,462	30
1969	1,578	32
1970	1,387	28
1971	1,570	32
1972	1,662	34
1973	1,804	37
1974	1,754	36
1975	1,835	37
1976	1,887	38
1977	1,820	37

Source: Registrar General's *Annual Statistical Reviews* (London: HMSO).

Damage to the brain and nervous tissue

People who drink very heavily are susceptible to brain damage, largely because of the impact of associated vitamin deficiencies, but also because of direct toxic action. Drinking usually has to be heavy and sustained for many years before this becomes a serious risk. It remains a mystery why many people who drink in such a manner do not damage their brains, while occasionally and unexpectedly a younger drinker becomes a casualty although his diet does not appear to have been particularly poor. The classical picture is that of *Korsakoff's psychosis*, a condition in which the patient has a catastrophic impairment of memory for recent events, while still remembering the more distant past with some clarity; together with this there are other signs of permanent loss of intellectual faculties (dementia). More often the picture is undramatic and non-specific, a feeling that concentration and memory are failing, a sense that mentally the person is 'losing his grip'. Various other brain syndromes are also known to occur. In its grossest form this relatively unusual but tragic type of damage results in most long-stay illness hospitals having some brain-damaged alcoholics as permanent patients who can only be given custodial care. Brain damage of this type is not reversible. It may well be that milder forms of alcohol-related damage to the brain are more common than is sometimes supposed, and contribute to the personality changes and the intractability of some chronic drinking.

The person who is drinking heavily can also develop a degeneration of the nerves which supply the limbs (peripheral neuritis), largely because of the associated vitamin deficiencies. The symptoms vary from the usually mild to the occasionally severe. The patient may have severe pain and great difficulty in walking. With treatment, and a reduction of his alcohol intake, recovery is usually complete.

Accidents and trauma

The relationship between drinking and road accidents has been discussed earlier in this chapter (pp. 68–73), and it is clear that there is an increased accident risk at levels of drinking well within the social-drinking range. There is not nearly so much hard information on the relationship between drinking levels and accidents in home or factory but, in one study of 300 consecutive fatalities from unintentional injuries, 30 per cent of those dying were known to be heavy drinkers or alcoholics. A report from the Western Infirmary in Glasgow has shown that almost 50 per cent of the admissions for head injuries are the result of assaults or falls while under the influence of alcohol and, at that hospital, admissions for such injuries are currently running at about 1,000 a year. In a later and more intensive study conducted at the Western Infirmary, 62 per cent of all males admitted with head injury were found to have alcohol in their blood, but it was not so much the presence but the level of alcohol which was astonishing: the mean blood alcohol level of those who had been drinking was 193 mg %, or two-and-a-half times the legal driving limit. Intoxication contributes significantly to accidental fires and fire deaths.

Damage to the foetus

Alcohol from the mother's bloodstream can pass through the placenta to reach the circulation of a baby in her uterus. There is no evidence that a mother who drinks moderate amounts of alcohol is going to do her baby any harm, but there is increasing evidence that a mother's heavy drinking can damage the foetus. What in this context is to be meant by 'moderate' as opposed to 'heavy' is as ever difficult to quantify precisely, but a level equivalent to, say, a couple of bottles of wine taken each day is getting into the danger area.

Babies affected by this sort of damage show a picture which has been termed 'the foetal alcohol syndrome'. In about 40 per cent of these cases there is mild to moderate mental retardation. The head tends to be abnormally small, and there may be congenital dislocation of the hips, congenital heart disease, and cleft palate or other congenital deformities.

This syndrome is being studied intensively in the United States. It is obvious that many women who drink heavily may have histories of poor nutrition, and be subject to various concurrent disadvantages. Only further research will be able to establish the precise contribution of the actual drinking.

Other physical problems related to heavy drinking

The paragraphs above have drawn attention to a number of specific complications. A highly compressed listing will now be given of the wider array of alcohol-related physical disabilities. Some of the items listed are fairly common, some fairly rare, and often it would be difficult to make any accurate statements on frequency of occurrence.

Alcohol can cause a degeneration of the heart muscle (cardiomyopathy) sometimes known as 'beer drinker's heart'. Inflammation and wasting of limb muscles can also occur (myopathy), and very rarely the overloading of the kidneys by the break-down products from the injured muscles can cause *renal failure* and death. Alcohol-induced inflammation of the pancreas (*pancreatitis*) is becoming increasingly common in this country. Acute alcoholic pancreatitis is predominantly a problem of young males – reports from Glasgow and Edinburgh have shown the seriousness of this complication in big cities where there is much heavy drinking in the young-male sector of the population. Pancreatitis can show up as an acute abdominal emergency, and the immediate mortality rate is about 9 per cent. The condition can also exist in a more chronic and smouldering form, or with many intermittent attacks. For a variety of reasons, *anaemia* may be associated with chronic heavy drinking. All manner of *vitamin deficiencies* can result from the accompanying dietary neglect, and heavy drinking must be one of the few remaining causes of beri-beri and scurvy in a country where nutritional standards are otherwise good. The general lowering of resistance means a risk of developing *tuberculosis* and, in a country where pulmonary TB has become increasingly rare, it is the down-and-out alcoholic who should still routinely have a chest X-ray. *Pneumonia* was traditionally a cause of death in heavy drinkers, but with the advent of antibiotics this should be rare. Attacks of *gout* can be brought on by heavy drinking. Withdrawal of alcohol when physical dependence is present can sometimes cause *epileptic convulsions*. *Delirium tremens* has been discussed under mental disabilities, but this is a physical as well as a mental illness, and certainly carries a risk of death, though this is much lower since the advent of modern treatments. Heavy drinking can precipitate a sudden lowering of blood sugar (*hypoglycaemia*), which produces symptoms that are readily confused with drunkenness, and which can be fatal. Alcohol may put diabetes out of control. At levels below those associated with alcohol dependence, there is an increased risk of *cancers of the oesophagus and pharynx*. Methyl alcohol, which is found in the surgical or methylated spirits that are drunk on Skid Row because of their cheapness, can cause *blindness*, nerve damage, and death. The structure of bones may be affected, with increased risk of *fractures*.

Prevalence of drinking problems in general hospitals

There does not appear to have been any very thorough attempt to screen hospitals in this country for the prevalence of drinking problems, and no doubt the figures would vary from hospital to hospital, and from ward to ward. The only British pilot study on which information is available gave the surprising proportion of 17 per cent for patients with alcohol problems in the beds of a general hospital. More comprehensive studies in Australia and the United States have suggested that, in those countries, up to 10 per cent of general hospital beds may be occupied because of disabilities related to alcohol.

Mortality studies

The question of whether teetotalism is associated with longevity has been much debated for well over a century. The best answer today would seem to be that moderate drinking does not carry any increased mortality risk, but that even the heavier types of acceptable social drinking carry some probability of a shortened life. What constitutes the cut-off point for safety is difficult to determine. A recent American government report fell back on what is known as 'Anstie's limit'. Anstie was a nineteenth-century British physician who proposed that the upper limit of safety for daily drinking was 3 oz of whisky, half a bottle of table wine, or a couple of pints of beer.

There is certainly a high mortality rate among heavy drinkers of the type who become clinically identified as alcoholics between findings from various countries, all of which show the very serious risks. A recent British publication reported a death-certificate search on a group of 935 patients who had been admitted to mental hospitals with a diagnosis of alcoholism, and who were followed after ten to fifteen years. Observed deathrate exceeded that which would have been expected in a general population group of the same age by a factor of 2·7 for men and 3·1 for women. Among subjects aged under forty years, this factor was 9·2. Considering different causes of death separately, the factor was 3·1 for tuberculosis, 1·7 for cancers, 22·7 for cirrhosis of the liver, and 24·9 for suicide. For accidents, poisoning, and violence combined, the factor was 15·8. To make this more clear, a 'factor of 3' would mean a mortality experience 300 per cent above that expected.

Some implications

We started this chapter by saying that its concern would be to display and examine the wide array of minor or major problems, mishaps, or damages in which drinking can be a causal or contributing factor. It was no part of that intention to overdramatize; and it is again worth emphasizing that the majority of people who drink will never come to any resultant harm. But on the basis of all the material accumulated in this chapter it must now be equally obvious that an accurate perspective must also have within its vision the fact that alcohol can result in disabilities of astonishing diversity, that these disabilities range from the trivial to the crippling or killing, and that frequently when actual figures can be produced the contributions that alcohol is making to varieties of incapacity is of major and surprising significance. It is necessary to insist that the picture must not be luridly exaggerated, but in reality the danger of imbalance largely lies in the other direction – most people in this country will today have only the haziest idea as to the true costs of excessive drinking in misery, illness, and death. Nor will they have any awareness of the costs in cash. Titbits of information on this or that aspect of the problem may find their way into public consciousness, but what is so lacking is an awareness of the startling pattern that emerges when all these separate bits of information are put together.

The total picture which is portrayed here must be made more common public property. We have presented evidence in Chapter 2 of this Report to support the optimistic belief that awareness over the past couple of decades has grown, but the level of awareness in general still falls far short of that which the facts properly demand. And the nature of those facts directly supports the argument that the need is for the widest possible *community* awareness, for it is every aspect of the community's life that is affected by excessive drinking. The scenes of our concern must embrace houses, streets, schools, offices and factories, and courts and prisons, as well as consulting rooms, casualty departments, and hospital wards. It must include the families and children, neighbours, workmates, and the other road users, who are inevitably and repeatedly going to be involved – for it is almost inconceivable that a drinking problem should affect but one actor, or only one actor and a doctor.

For the helping professions and the design of services the evidence implies a need for help which must be able to respond to an extraordinarily wide variety of problems, and which should often be able to deal with the alcohol issue within a wider and unspecialized context of causes and disorders. It must be obvious that a specialized treatment service which sits back and waits for the problem to present itself as 'alcoholism' will only be able to make a tiny contribution to what is really needed.

A further implication relates to prevention. What has to be prevented is clearly not one single type of process, one disease entity of alcoholism, or anything of unitary causation, but a mass of problems of varied origin in the genesis of which alcohol plays a greater or lesser contributing part. The awarenesses that come from this type of review must lead to broad and multiple preventive strategies.

The final implication to be drawn must be that there are still manifest gaps in the evidence. So far, there has been little in the way of purposive and comprehensive monitoring of the social, health, and economic costs of excessive drinking. Small pieces of evidence from that city or this hospital, supported perhaps by mortality statistics or crime statistics, allow some sort of patchwork to be put together. But the information is often incomplete, and it is most often available only because of the chance zeal of some particular investigator rather than because anyone was demanding to know. We should demand to know more often and more completely.

6

The causes of
harmful drinking

In Chapter 4 the nature of alcohol dependence was considered, and in Chapter 5 we have looked at the wide range of disabilities that can result from excessive use of alcohol. The question which has now to be tackled is *why* people drink in such a manner as to induce dependence, or to incur disability, or both. The reasons for asking this question are eminently practical, for only when we understand why people drink harmfully does it become possible to suggest appropriate steps leading to prevention or to treatment. In this chapter the aim will therefore be to relate the evidence to its practical implications, although these implications will be dealt with more specifically in the final chapter.

There is certainly no single answer to the question of why people drink, or drink excessively, and a considerable number of interacting factors must combine to explain why any particular person drinks in his chosen fashion. It is useful to group all these factors under the two broad headings of *social* and *personal* (allowing for some overlap), and this is the division that we shall employ here.

Social factors and the development of harmful drinking

*The relationship between overall national drinking levels
and alcohol-related disability*

This is a matter of the utmost importance to understanding the social processes that can play a part in the genesis of alcoholism. What can be asserted is that if the average man or woman begins to drink more (that is, if the national *per capita* alcohol consumption rises), then the number of people who damage themselves by their drinking will also increase. Similarly, if there is a decrease in *per capita* consumption, there will be fewer people in the country damaged by drinking. 'Normal drinking' and excessive drinking are not two distinct species of behaviour, with entirely different determinants.

The implication of this statement must be that the amount a nation drinks is a matter of health concern – the citizens of any country cannot expect to drink more each year without each year having more alcohol-related casualties in their midst. This statement runs contrary to the comfortable and previously accepted view that alcoholism is a disease from which a minority of unfortunate people are destined to suffer, whatever the general availability of alcohol, while the majority are thought to be inherently immune from alcohol-related problems, whatever its availability. The older view was attractive; it invited the notion that if drink is cheaper and the pubs are open for longer hours, then all of us who are normal drinkers can enjoy more of the good things in life, with no harm done. 'Common sense' is often called upon to bolster up this position. Surely the result of more liberal availability of alcohol would be that the mass of people who are safely enjoying their drink would just have the occasional extra pint at the end of the evening, or a bottle of wine with their dinner a little more frequently? Surely, too, the impact of making alcohol less easily available and diminishing the *per capita* consumption would be that ordinary drinkers would cut down, while the person who is heavily dependent on alcohol would somehow find a way, by drinking a cheaper brand of liquor, or by further impoverishing his family, to continue his level of intake?

This seemingly common-sense line of argument turns out to be mistaken. A mass of evidence, culled from international analyses of drinking data, supports the assertion that shifts in average *per capita* consumption will be accompanied by shifts in indices of alcohol-related disabilities, in the same direction. Moreover, the shift is not simply proportionate: a given change in average consumption will be accompanied by a disproportionately magnified change of casualty rates. Even rather small shifts in national consumption of alcohol have, therefore, from the health point of view, to be taken seriously because of their unexpectedly large effects on the casualty rates.

The statistical treatment of the relevant data involves complex procedures, and there are many pitfalls. This is not the context in which to examine in detail the original data and methods of analysis that have been employed; it would be better to suggest that anyone specially interested in the technicalities should refer to the bibliography. But in summary it would be fair to say that the evidence, both from time-trend analyses for individual countries (for periods of decreasing as well as increasing consumption), and from between-country comparisons, gives strong empirical support to the statement that *per capita* consumption and health damage from alcohol go hand in hand, up hill and down dale.

This summary interpretation of the evidence does not suggest that there is a scientific *law* – there may well be, in some countries and over particular periods, circumstances which result in trends that go against the expected trend (over certain periods, the UK figures have undoubtedly been out of step with the expectations). Moreover, it may be the case that some, but not all, disabilities show this relationship with average consumption, or show it in different degree. Cirrhosis deaths and deaths from some other alcohol-related causes have tended to fit the expectations rather well, but we lack evidence about the relationship between average consumption and social disruptions related to alcohol.

Given that the facts generally run contrary to the 'common-sense' assumptions either that making alcohol more available mainly results in more normal drinking, or that less alcohol availability does not inhibit the excessive drinker, where do these intuitive expectations go wrong? The explanation is probably that in any population there exists a small percentage of people whose drinking is on the borderline between relatively safe, and harmful drinking. However, in a population of millions, a 'small percentage' will imply hundreds of thousands of people. If for that sector of drinkers alcohol is made more available, in a borderline drinker the increase may be just sufficient to damage some tissues of his body, or crucially to impair the capacity to work, or to make the marriage intolerable for the spouse. A further grave possibility is that the borderline drinker will increase his consumption just sufficiently to induce the dependence syndrome.

What also has to be explained is why a reduction in *per capita* consumption usually results in a fall in casualty rates (without a prolonged time gap). This becomes more understandable if it is realized that a great deal of alcohol-related damage is contributed by people who are not heavily alcohol dependent, and who are likely in varying degree to be sensitive to changes in availability. Furthermore, it is a misunderstanding to suppose that even someone with a severe and fully developed dependence syndrome will be *entirely* unresponsive to general constraints on availability: he may not cut down on his drinking dramatically, but might for instance do so sufficiently to prevent or postpone the development of cirrhosis.

The data, their statistical handling, and the argument about their inner meaning, continue to be matters for highly technical debate, but there is an essential simplicity in the message which comes through. Take any population, increase its average *per capita* consumption, and it is likely that everyone will move up a little, but a disproportionate percentage will then move up far enough to be in danger. Decrease consumption, and it is probable that everyone moves down a little, and a disproportionate percentage will move out of the danger zone.

What may not always be realized is that considerable shifts in national alcohol consumption are indeed possible over a period of years. *Table 4* gives data calculated for five-year periods from 1885 to 1930, to show both an initial rise and a later fall in alcohol consumption. The rise was during the late Victorian period. The fall started to occur before the 1914–18 war, accelerated greatly during the war period, and continued during the subsequent economic depression. The right-hand column shows very roughly parallel changes in an index of alcohol-related mortality. Too much should not be made of the precise details of this table, for computation of alcohol consumption involves a number of arbitrary assumptions, and the index of mortality is also not very satisfactory. However, it is reasonable to conclude that, over this period, alcohol consumption varied by a factor of about two-and-a-half (4·2 in 1895–1900, to 1·6 in 1930–4), while coincidentally the alcoholism mortality rate fell by a factor of rather less than four. Very clearly the level of the country's alcoholism is far from being fixed once and for all, but must be open to influences by all manner of forces.

Table 4 UK *per capita* alcohol consumption and alcohol-related mortality for quinquennial periods 1885 to 1930

Quinquenium	*Index of annual per capita alcohol consumption (Gallons of proof spirit)*	*Index of alcohol-related mortality (Annual deaths per million living certified as due to chronic alcoholism, DTs, or cirrhosis)*
1885–9	3·8	154
1890–4	4·0	168
1895–9	4·2	182
1900–4	4·1	193
1905–9	3·6	156
1910–14	3·4	131
1915–19	2·3	81
1920–4	2·3	59
1925–9	2·0	55
1930–4	1·6	42

Turning to more recent times, an analysis of the UK *per capita* consumption of alcohol from 1950–76 showed a rise of 87 per cent, and drinking is once more in a period of fairly consistent upward climb. *Table 5* gives the relevant data, and shows in particular the extraordinary recent increase in wine drinking. The

Table 5 United Kingdom consumption of alcoholic beverages
1950–76

Year	Beer (Million bulk barrels)	Spirits (Million proof gallons)	Wine (British and imported) (Million gallons)	Annual per capita consumption of persons aged 15 years and over (Litres of absolute alcohol)
1950	26	10	13	5·2
1951	26	10	15	5·3
1952	26	10	14	5·3
1953	25	10	15	5·1
1954	25	11	17	5·2
1955	25	12	18	5·3
1956	25	12	19	5·3
1957	25	13	20	5·3
1958	25	13	20	5·3
1959	26	14	23	5·6
1960	27	15	27	5·8
1961	29	16	28	6·2
1962	29	16	30	6·1
1963	29	17	33	6·2
1964	30	18	37	6·5
1965	30	18	36	6·5
1966	30	18	38	6·5
1967	31	18	42	6·7
1968	31	19	46	7·0
1969	33	18	45	7·0
1970	34	20	46	7·3
1971	35	21	54	7·7
1972	35	24	62	7·7
1973	37	30	78	7·9
1974	39	33	83	8·9
1975	40	32	78	9·4
1976	41	36	81	9·7

Source: HM Customs and Excise Annual Reports (London: HMSO) for data in first three columns. The *per capita* consumption (4th column) is based on the assumption that beer on average contains 4% alcohol, spirits 39·9% alcohol, and wine 16%: these figures can only be approximate. The relevant population base for each year was gained from the series Annual Abstract of Statistics (London: HMSO), and between censuses involves projections.

94

impact of economic recession may, though, be expected to push the curve temporarily downwards again and there are recent signs that this has been happening. It is dangerous to read too much into fluctuations over comparatively short periods.

Recent trends in our own country's alcohol consumption must be put in the context of the experience of other western countries, and *Table 6* gives instances of a number of nations which have during recent years shown a positive shift in consumption, and of one country (France) which has shown a fall.

Table 6 Change in *per capita* consumption of alcohol in a number of European countries

Country	per capita *consumption in litres absolute alcohol*		% *change*
	1950–2	1968–70	
Austria	5·4	10·8	100
Belgium	6·6	8·4	27
Denmark	4·0	7·0	75
Finland	2·2	4·4	100
France	17·6	16·1	−9
Germany (Federal Republic)	3·6	10·1	181
Italy	9·4	13·7	46
Netherlands	1·9	5·3	179
Norway	2·1	3·5	67
United Kingdom	4·9	6·2	27

Source: Bruun, K. *et al.* (1975) *Alcohol Control Policies in Public Health Perspective*. Helsinki: Finnish Foundation for Alcohol Studies.

Changes in British drinking are therefore part of a wider international process. With the growth of European economic cooperation and the reduction of tariff barriers, consumption may be expected to level out at a new high, with differences between countries not so marked as has traditionally been the case.

This discussion has a direct bearing on health concerns. The chain of argument runs as follows: the alcohol-consumption level of a country is linked to the alcohol-related casualty rates of that country (give or take a little, and without setting up any invariable 'natural law', or supposing that all alcohol-related disabilities rise or fall in the same way). Moreover, a given change in consumption will generally result in a more-than-proportionate change in the rates for disabilities. Historical as well as cross-national evidence shows that possible variations in consumption levels are really quite substantial, and recent figures suggest that the United Kingdom, along with other countries, is now on an upward swing. It therefore becomes especially important to understand what causes such changes in consumption levels, since these could be enormously relevant to preventive policies. In the broadest sense the influences that are responsible for the ebb and flow must be social ones. Some of the possible social determinants must therefore be considered.

Social factors determining national levels of drinking

The relevant influences can be divided into economic influences (pricing) and *formal* controls (licensing) on the one hand, and *informal* controls (custom and cultural expectations) on the other. It may be useful at first to consider these influences separately, but the way in which they interact must also be taken into account.

There is evidence to suggest that the relative price of drink is a potent factor affecting consumption. If drink is cheaper, in terms of the corrected value of money which must take account both of wage levels and inflationary effects on the real value of money, then the average person will drink rather more. Little detailed economic analysis of the price/consumption relationship has so far been published in Britain, and there are pitfalls here for the unwary, but *Figure 2* (which is reproduced from a recent research report by Drs Semple and Yarrow) plots whisky consumption in the UK against corrected price of a bottle of whisky expressed as a percentage of disposable income. 'Personal disposable income' is the remainder of earned and unearned income after deduction of taxes, National Insurance contributions, etc.

The relationship that is revealed is a strong inverse correlation: if whisky gets X per cent cheaper then the average citizen drinks proportionately more whisky, and vice versa. This finding is by no means exceptional. There is now a mass of evidence from the analysis of data from other countries which confirms this fundamental relationship between the 'real' price of alcohol, and consumption. When price goes up, consumption falls; when price goes down, consumption rises. Alcohol consumption seems to be responsive to price in roughly the same way as are many other marketed commodities. In summary, although there may

Figure 2   *Whisky consumption against price per bottle (UK 1950–70)*

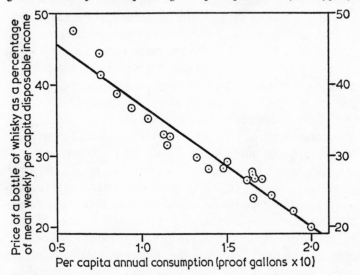

be exceptions to every rule, it can today be accepted that the real price of alcohol profoundly influences the nation's drinking.

Turning to formal controls, it seems likely that the licensing apparatus is also of some importance. This system is governed by a complex body of legislation which has grown piecemeal, and been much tinkered with over time. It controls such matters as the granting of licences for sales 'on' or 'off' the premises, opening hours, the minimum age of drinking, and so on. To demonstrate the relationship between control legislation and alcohol consumption is more difficult than between consumption and price: in this instance, the situation does not offer the possibility of a neat analysis using gradual variations over time in two readily measurable variables (as with price and consumption). All that can be done is to try to interpret the significance of the various 'experiments of nature' which occur when this or that element of the licensing regulations is altered. The difficulty is that such elements are not often altered one at a time, and there may be other major events taking place concurrently: a war, a slump, or perhaps a large price change. Some instances can however be identified where a radical alteration in licensing has been followed so immediately and by so large an alteration in *per capita* drinking that a confident conclusion can be drawn. Such an event was recently seen in Finland. In 1969 the Finnish Government abruptly relaxed previously very restrictive licensing controls: in 1968 there were 1,600 shops, restaurants, or bars selling alcohol, and by 1970 the number of licensed outlets had dramatically increased to over 21,000. *Per capita* alcohol consumption rose by about 50 per cent over these two years. The attempt made in our own country to control 'the liquor problem' in the years 1914–18 was in some ways the obverse of the recent Finnish experiment: a whole range of government measures was aimed at cutting down the harm which drinking appeared to be causing to the nation's productivity. But this was also an instance where a good many other things were going on at the same time – a package of restrictive licensing, diversion of raw materials from brewing, men called up into the armed forces, and much else besides. It is impossible to make any firm assertion as to which factor contributed most. What is not in doubt is that between 1913 and 1917 spirit consumption fell by 55 per cent, beer by 56 per cent, and wine by 35 per cent. At the same time, wages reached a new high.

From these two dramatic instances, to which others could be added, we must conclude that average alcohol consumption can in some circumstances be directly influenced by controls. The 'natural experiment' is however not usually of such dimensions, and instances could no doubt be quoted where limited changes in licensing seem to have had no detectable influence on consumption. It has been argued, therefore, that licensing revisions affect levels of drinking only if they are very considerable. In those terms, the Finnish experiment only produced such extraordinary results because the baseline was one of severe restriction and the change an unusually large and abrupt relaxation. The argument would run that, by comparison, opening Scottish pubs for an hour longer in the evening would be a measure of such small significance (and one starting from a very un-Finnish baseline) that the impact would hardly be discernible. However, it could alternatively be argued that, if a big change in control policy produces a big change in consumption, a smaller policy change is quite likely to produce a real but smaller change in consumption, albeit one which may be difficult to detect.

The contention that relaxation of licensing laws is not inimical to health interests has recently in some quarters been pressed very strongly, and it has even been proposed that relaxation of licensing could be positively *beneficial* to public health. The argument has been extended in this way in the recent Scottish report on liquor licensing (the Clayson Committee). That committee took the view that by extending licensing hours people would not have to drink so quickly, and by widening the range of licensed premises men would be able to drink with their families. The general belief was that liberalization of the licensing laws could lead to drinking less for the sake of intoxication and in a generally more civilized manner, so that new and healthier patterns would emerge with drinking integrated with other social activities. Others have expressed the fear that new drinking patterns would simply be added to old patterns, rather than old patterns being eliminated.

To be dogmatic as to the influence of formal controls on alcohol consumption would in present circumstances be wrong, and the evidence is not so clear-cut here as with price. At least in the short term, changes in Scottish licensing controls have been accompanied by a fall in the number of arrests for public drunkenness, but the influence of background economic forces on wage levels would certainly have to be taken into account before conclusions could be drawn in either direction. A reasonably fair conclusion would probably be that extreme relaxation of formal controls is very risky, while a less extreme relaxation will have uncertain consequences on health: it is probably quite accurate to describe even minor relaxations as 'a bit of a gamble'. Such evidence as exists certainly offers little or nothing to support the optimistic contention that relaxation is actually likely to benefit health, and that particular line of argument seems to be rather dangerous. The significance of licensing as a possible instrument of public health is an issue that will be returned to later.

Turning now to *informal controls*, what influences can be identified as bearing on *per capita* consumption? So far, the factors which have been examined are those which could be regarded as rather mechanical. Because pricing and licensing are potentially subject to manipulation in the cause of health, there has been great interest in recent years in researching their effect on consumption. However, literature which has shown the importance of more general and subtle sociocultural influences on the manner in which a population uses alcohol should also receive attention. One country may be renowned as 'a nation of drunkards' while another is remarked on for its abstemiousness, and this not only because of national differences in the prices of alcohol or the licensing laws, but also because of fundamentally different national attitudes to drinking. For instance, the eighteenth-century excesses of Gin Lane might be seen as rooted not only in the cheapness of liquor – 'drunk for a penny, dead drunk for tuppence' – and in the relative laxity of formal licensing controls at the time, but also in the breakdown of informal controls due to the social disruptions of the Industrial Revolution.

The idea of 'informal control' needs to be examined. The phrase suggests that any society will have social customs regarding the proper amount to drink (by whom, and in what circumstances), and these informal controls, though not published or proclaimed as a set of rules, may often be as potent as any Act of Parliament in controlling the population's drinking. The quantity which a person drinks on any occasion will be determined not only by the amount of money he has in his pocket and by licensing laws which make it more (or less) easy for him to purchase a drink, but also by whether social mores deem this to be an appropriate time of day for drinking, whether the mores suggest it is generally appropriate when drinking to take alcohol in moderate quantities or to drink to inebriety, and so on. The appropriateness of drinking behaviour, as of table manners, is socially determined. Drinking is a social act, whether it takes place in public or private; it is linked to social definitions of appropriate drinking and forms part of the context of more general social values, attitudes, and expectations regarding self-indulgence, emotional show, loss of self-control, and so on. The powerful reality of informal social controls of drinking can be identified in all societies, both complex and pre-literate. When considering the practicalities of prevention, the extent to which informal controls can usefully be strengthened has to be examined closely.

But a real understanding of the inner meaning of *Tables 4* and *5* requires not the listing of *separate* influences but an awareness of the likely *interaction* between these influences. That the average person in this country drinks more alcohol today than he did fifteen years ago may be due to price changes, may possibly in some measure reflect the influence of small changes in formal controls (the growth, for instance, of supermarket sales), and may also have been affected by changing social trends and life styles. But in reality these different elements do not stand in isolation. That drink has become relatively cheap, and readily purchasable by the woman who is doing the family shopping, will change social attitudes as to what is appropriate drinking. Social attitudes towards drinking will influence official policies on pricing: drink is seemingly accepted as a necessity, and forms part of the cost-of-living index. Higher wages may mean more Continental holidays and a greater taste for wine, as well as having more disposable income with which to buy it.

The essential point is therefore that *per capita* consumption is determined by a network of causes, and not just by one dominant element or by an array of quite separate elements. Even if the system is difficult to analyse in all its dynamic complexity, we are certainly today able to recognize some of its major elements, and to make some informed guesses as to the likely interactions; and we are undoubtedly forced to an awareness that this system exerts a subtle but enormously powerful influence on the population's drinking.

Social factors which help to explain why some groups drink more than others

Up to now we have been looking at social factors and drinking largely in terms of very broad national influences. Much can be established by analysis at this level, but it is also necessary to probe deeper, and to discover the more personal correlates of lighter or heavier drinking among social groupings and subcultures. It is here that survey data begin to illuminate the matter.

The first clear finding from surveys in which a sample of the population is asked what they drink and why they drink is that no one person is abstinent, or drinks at a particular level, for just one reason: quite inevitably we again face the need to think in terms of multiple and interactive causes. A host of influences have their meeting point in the individual's drinking habits. The broad influence of informal social controls on the population has already been noted, but it is also necessary to look at the way in which those controls affect different groups within the population in different ways. Social controls differentiate, for instance, between the sexes, and permit men to drink more than women: traditionally, part of the definition of manliness in many cultures is that the real man is a drinking man. A woman who drinks heavily is much more readily subjected to disapproval. Society also ordains (partly by convention and expectation, partly by the distribution of spending power), that people of different age will drink differently. Children are expected not to drink or to drink very little, and one proof of growing independence is the right to buy your own drink or go into a pub. The young adult is looked on somewhat askance but also with amused indulgence when he occasionally drinks quite wildly. The middle years are the years of settled socialized drinking, while the old-age pensioner is expected just to drink his quiet pint.

There are, of course, variations in these social expectations even within the same country: different social classes, ethnic groups, and religious denominations will all present their own patterns. City, town, and village – all may drink differently. However, the broad pattern of sex and age relationships is probably fairly accurately reflected in *Table 7*, which gives data from a survey conducted in a London suburb.

The cumulative influence of sex and age is sharply illustrated by contrasting the 55 per cent of young men (aged eighteen to thirty-four) who are moderate or heavy drinkers with the 2 per cent of women aged fifty or over who drink to that extent. Such findings may so much agree with common-sense expectation that

Table 7 Percentage of sample in various drinking categories by age and sex (Survey in Camberwell, London, 1966)

Drinking category	Age groups					
	18–34		35–49		50+	
	Men (n= 119)	Women (n = 124)	Men (n= 132)	Women (n= 142)	Men (n = 153)	Women (n= 252)
	%	%	%	%	%	%
Abstainers	4	5	4	5	12	15
Occasional drinkers	14	41	17	33	20	35
Light drinkers	27	43	38	52	38	48
Moderate drinkers	34	11	23	9	24	2
Heavy drinkers	21	0	18	1	6	0

they can rather too easily be dismissed as 'obvious'; on the other hand, it is exactly such obvious facts which should alert our curiosity as to the nature of such astonishingly powerful social processes. It is social custom – the way society orders the individual drinker's practices, attitudes, expectations, and values – which produces the striking contrast between the drinking of those younger men and those older women, rather than any influence of law or formal regulation.

The influence of an individual's occupation is another factor which has an effect on his drinking. This can be exerted in several ways. The most direct influence will be when the job makes alcohol specially available to him at little or no cost – the hotel chef or kitchen porter who is given as much drink as he wants, the barman who is repeatedly being stood drinks by his customers, the brewery worker who is granted or knows how to 'fiddle' a daily ration of beer, and so on. Some people in such occupations may of course be attracted to work where alcohol is available since they are drinking heavily already: the barman's choice of occupation may, for instance, be as much an effect of his drinking as a continuing support of his habit. The influence of occupation may also work in many other powerful but less direct ways, as in the cases of the executive or the travelling sales-man with expense-account entertaining, the unmarried itinerant labourer whose only leisure activity is drinking with other men in the pub, the worker in the printing trade who is exposed to strong occupational traditions of drinking, the actor or enter-tainer, or the street photographer who always goes to the pub when it rains.

Perhaps equally obvious to anyone who reflects on his own or his neighbour's drinking are the findings that, by and large, people drink more when they have higher earnings, if they had parents who drank heavily, or if they are of Scottish or Irish origin. The Camberwell survey found no Jewish person in the two heaviest drinking categories.

Behind such correlates must lie many complexities. Society defines appropriate drinking occasions, symbolic meanings of alcohol, its ritual uses, and medicinal applications. Drinking is the thing to do at weddings (but not at Baptist weddings). You drink at a football match, but rather more moderately at the opera. Whisky is good for a cold, brandy is sent for when some-one faints. When a bargain is struck, it calls for a drink. This meal needs a bottle of wine – but other people would never drink with their meals. If you won't let me stand you a drink it may be an insult and there's awkwardness if you ask for a soft drink, while it is the role of the senior and not the junior person to stand the drink. A 'party' means a drinking party, except for children. 'Drinking' means drinking alcohol.

Environmental stress

Any environment which imposes continued stress on an indi-vidual can invite a risk of heavy drinking. A marriage which is going through difficulties, a bad patch of business worries, concern over physical health, the difficult readjustments of moving to a new town or a new country, too much demand or the sudden withdrawal of demands on giving up a job, can all generate unpleasant feelings which the individual may then cope with by drinking. He does not necessarily say to himself consciously, 'I am being made anxious by the threat of bankruptcy and another drink will soothe those feelings,' but nonetheless, and over a surprisingly short time, the story frequently seems to be of a rapid increase in drinking having occurred during a difficult period of life, with the drinking often then remaining at the new level when the situation is later resolved. 'Stress' is a concept of rather loose meaning, and what may be stressful to one person need not necessarily be stressful to another person in exactly the same situation. As well as the immediate types of environmental stresses which have been mentioned above, there is some evidence that very general aspects of the threats and insecurities of the larger environment can influence drinking: anthropological studies suggest that such considerations may be important in contributing to different levels of drinking in primitive societies, while recent research suggests that in the USA economic slump may be associated with a rise in cirrhosis rates.

Social factors and the way people behave when intoxicated

Not only will social factors influence the likelihood of excessive drinking, but there will also be social forces which indicate the way in which the individual should behave when he has been drinking, and these second-order influences will contribute to the likelihood of excessive drinking leading to actual harm. Social influences will, for instance, have played a large part in determining that at a wedding the bride's father has drunk a great deal. Secondary social influences will have an important part to play in determining whether or not he then gets into his car and drives himself away from the wedding reception, with risk to life and limb. Again, the influences are both formal and informal: there is the attempt at formal constraint in terms of drunk driving legislation and its enforcement, while there will be informal influences exerted perhaps by the man's wife, or by other guests at the wedding, who will try to persuade him to let someone else do the driving. Once more, formal and informal controls will interact, for the existence of the legislation will influence the way in which other people informally respond to that man.

Drinking and driving provides a clear example of these types of social influence, but many other forms of 'drunken comportment' must be similarly influenced. In certain cultures or subcultures violence may for instance be seen as a likely consequence of drinking and so violence will ensue; hence the bar-room brawl, or the drunken man hitting his wife. In other groups, drinking may be seen as in no way associated with violence, although there may be argument, loquacity, intimate revelation, and boastfulness. However much the bishop drinks in his club with his fellow clerics or argues over the port, and whatever their various temperaments, no-one would in that setting expect a drunken punch-up to be the likely outcome.

When considering how alcohol-related problems can best be prevented, ways in which controls on drunken behaviour may be strengthened will therefore clearly have to be taken into account, as well as primary social influences on the likelihood of excessive drinking itself.

Individual factors and the causes of harmful drinking

Having devoted considerable space to an examination of the many interacting social influences that can play a part in the genesis of harmful drinking, this new heading does not mean that all the previous discussion can now be laid aside while an entirely separate and alternative line of argument is developed. On the contrary, what must be stressed is the complementary nature of the social and personal explanations. In the discussion of individual factors which follows, what has to be borne in mind is that the individual, with all his personal propensities, lives in a social setting which will greatly determine which propensities are in fact developed.

Genetic considerations: the nature-nurture controversy

A common observation is that people with serious drinking problems quite often have a parent, brother, sister, or other relative who has experienced the same sort of problem. According to recent American studies, about one-third of male first-degree relatives of an alcoholic are likely to have a drinking problem, and this is a much higher rate than would be expected by chance. Put simply, alcoholism runs in families, specially in the males of the family.

Two different types of explanation could be offered for this observation. The one which has generally found most favour is the postulate that parental example is a potent influence – the alcoholic's son becomes an alcoholic much as the architect's son or daughter may take up the father's trade. A piece of research which has often been quoted as supporting this family-environment type of explanation is a study published over thirty years ago by Dr Ann Roe. She went through the records of a child fostering agency in New York, and was able to find thirty-six cases where the biological father was an excessive drinker, and the child had been taken out of the original home before the age of ten years. A control group of fostered children from homes where there was no record of excessive drinking was also studied. The follow-up to an age of about thirty showed that there was no difference between these two fostered groups in adult drinking behaviour.

The alternative explanation for the drinking problem of the alcoholic's son is genetic. The great bulk of evidence relating to social influences on drinking has frequently been interpreted as suggesting that there can be little room left for genetic explanations, but there is of course no good reason to consider the sociocultural and genetic explanations as mutually exclusive and opposed. Over recent years there has been a renewed interest in human genetic studies of drinking, and so much careful research has now been published on this topic that it cannot safely be ignored. There is also a considerable literature on the genetics of drinking in laboratory animals.

The most recent major genetic research on alcoholism has been that conducted by Dr Donald Goodwin and his American and Danish colleagues. Their work is based on the records of adopted children in Copenhagen. The findings include the fact that the sons of alcoholics, when adopted away from the original home in early life, are significantly more likely to develop drinking problems than the sons of non-alcoholics adopted away (18 per cent versus 5 per cent). Furthermore, the sons of alcoholics who are adopted away are not significantly less likely to develop drinking problems than their brothers who are left at home to grow up in the presence of the drinking father (25 per cent versus 17 per cent).

Any idea that genetic theories are to be dismissed easily is thus heavily challenged. The genetic influence could operate in a number of different ways. There might be inheritance of a taste or 'appetite' for drinking, or conversely a protective inheritance of a tendency to develop particularly adverse reactions to heavy drinking – a propensity perhaps to become rather easily nauseated. Yet another possibility would be of inheritance mediated indirectly through personality predisposition or depressive disorders.

Genetic studies of drinking and excessive drinking should be placed in a context of understanding provided by the larger background of general genetic research. It is common to find that *some* genetic contribution can be established for many aspects of human attributes or disorders (ranging from musical ability to duodenal ulcers), and drinking is unlikely to be the exception. What is much more difficult to establish is the precise degree of genetic contribution, the manner in which the genetic influence acts, and the extent to which genetic predisposition may be modified by environment. Present evidence suggests that the links between the alcoholic father and his son with a drinking problem will not be found in any very simple genetic mechanisms, such as operate for instance in the inheritance of colour blindness.

One important cause of excessive drinking is that personality predisposes people to such behaviour. To take an example, an ambitious woman who was striving and successful, but who despite outward appearances was lacking in social confidence, saw the origins of her drinking thus:

'I suppose I first discovered that a drink would *do* something for me pretty early on. At seventeen or eighteen I was quite desperately shy and it would be real pain for me to have to go out to parties or out on a date, or join in any sort of social gathering. But then I found that if I could get a couple of drinks down I'd be much less tense, really able to join the gang. For a good few years I just used drink that way, as a tranquillizer to get me through social situations. Then when I was about thirty my career began to go well and I got promotion, and was working very hard, and the job itself began to mean a lot of socializing; I didn't want to say "I can't do it, don't give me that promotion." That's when my drinking began to take off . . .'

The expectation that personality can be one of the determinants of excessive drinking is supported by a variety of research findings and also by a mass of everyday observations.

One very important line of research has been the community sample survey, which employs door-to-door interviews and which can provide information on the relationships between quantity drunk, reasons given for drinking, problems with drinking, and aspects of personality. A consistent finding is that heavier drinkers (and by implication people who have more problems with drinking), tend to be found among those who are using alcohol for 'personal' reasons. By this is meant the use of alcohol to relieve 'bad nerves' or tension, or restlessness or boredom, or as something that helps to forget one's worries. Not surprisingly, people who are using alcohol particularly to relieve such feelings are, in general, likely also to be particularly possessed of such feelings, and many different tests of personality point in this direction. The suggestion is therefore that vulnerable personalities will find alcohol functionally useful as a nerve drug, which in turn will lead to heavy drinking and consequently to troubles with drinking.

But are we right in supposing that personality predisposes to harmful drinking, or is the contrary explanation the correct one – that excessive drinking is itself the cause of the abnormalities detected by those personality measures? Heavy drinking can certainly result in 'bad nerves' (see p. 74). The obvious way to meet this difficulty is to set up studies which follow a large sample of children forward into adult life, and which could determine whether any identifiable personality characteristics are predictive of development of later drinking problems. Such an approach should also be able to identify any predictive features in the early home environment and family constellation which are associated with later risk of alcoholism. An alternative attack on the question is to take a sample of adults and then trace backwards for information independently recorded earlier in their lives. A number of such researches have been reported, but here also there are limitations which have to be borne in mind. Such work strictly speaks only of predictive factors found in the particular samples studied, and research has generally concentrated on the more disadvantaged sort of child from a rather poor background. Nearly all the relevant work comes from the USA.

Clinical experience offers various ideas as to psychological predisposition to alcoholism, and there is no one psychological explanation of these problems, and certainly no unique 'alcoholic personality'. On the contrary there are a great many personality traits which can (given the circumstances) predispose to excessive drinking, and any of these traits can be found in degree rather than as absolutely present or absent. None of these personality characteristics are unique to people with drinking problems. One person may develop heavy dependence on alcohol rather directly because of major abnormalities in personality, while another individual with much the same type of drinking problem can be a well-integrated person with minor vulnerabilities, who has been exposed to great pressure of circumstances. Psychiatric thinking would today give no support to the simple view that personality abnormality is the complete explanation of excessive drinking.

The range of ideas that psychiatry offers for understanding the individual case includes explanations in terms of immaturity of personality, defect in self-esteem, dependence conflict, the excessive drinking that is a hostile or revengeful act in the person with strong aggressive tendencies, the drinking that is a more or less purposeful act of 'chronic suicide', the person who is using drink to achieve a sense of acute excitement – a 'high' state – not otherwise available to him, or the undisciplined drinking that is symptomatic of a personality generally weak in self-control or in responsiveness to the feelings of others.

In essence what has to be realized is that drinking can change the inner state of a person who is in any of many ways discontented with that state: it can set up a feeling tone of pleasure, tranquillity, or elation. 'I reach the ceiling of my world,' one man explained. Instead of strenuous and patient effort to achieve some distant goal, a drinking session can confer immediate and almost effortless satisfactions on someone whose personality otherwise makes it difficult to find contentment.

To take one clinical example in a little more detail, the excessive drinker who lacks self-confidence, has little self-esteem, and may even be disgusted at himself, can sometimes be very readily identified. Often such a person will have been deprived of affection in childhood, sometimes frankly neglected, or even brutally mistreated. Women may describe cold, unloving mothers who expected the worst of them, or stepfathers who never regarded them affectionately; men may have been physically assaulted by parents, or made to feel wicked or depraved. 'Self-punitiveness' is a characteristic of such alcoholics as these, apparently long predating the onset of dependence: for them alcohol gives respite from mental self-flagellation, and from a pervading sense of insufficiency and inferiority.

A second example is of a very different type of person quite free of self-loathing and not troubled in personal relations – the self-indulgent individual, who was pampered in childhood by doting or anxious parents. He may have been the only son, or the youngster for whom everything was done and on whom few demands were imposed, or the sheltered being who never really needed to fend for himself. Such a person can find that the harsh realities of work, personal relations, and marriage add up to a bleak vista of obligations and responsibilities. These he may meet more or less effectively, but he may also discover that drinking can confer a mental holiday. When under the influence of alcohol to the right extent, exciting reveries can be summoned to transform mundane existence.

In treatment, the hedonistic patient who has been seeking euphoria seems to do rather better than the self-punitive alcoholic who lets up on himself only when drinking.

These two types of drinker have been discussed to illustrate how differently the personality can be organized in the stage before heavy drinking develops. The view of alcoholism that is to be gained by listening to people who have themselves tried to understand what it was in their personalities that was predisposing to heavy drinking is that there is indeed a range of moderately useful generalizations, but there is also the ultimate truth that no two cases are alike.

Psychiatric illness as an individual predisposing factor

In the preceding section we have looked at the ways in which personality may predispose to excessive drinking. By 'personality' is meant the sort of person, the cast of temperament, the sum of psychological attributes – the variations on the normal themes. Less common than personality predisposition or variation in psychological constitution are those instances where discreet and diagnosable mental illness underlies the development of a drinking problem. If some of these illnesses were more adequately treated (or after-care more effectively organized), a contribution might be made to the prevention of drinking problems, and in some instances an underlying mental illness might point to the type of treatment that may be needed.

Perhaps the most common association is with *depressive illness*. By depressive illness is meant here not the tendency on occasion to feel a bit down in the dumps, which is in different degree part of everyone's experience and for some people a major and life-long temperamental problem which may be associated with other difficulties in adjustment, but the definitely recognizable mental illness often developing in the previously normal person. It can be a response to stress, bereavement, the menopause, retirement, or it can be quite unheralded. The person suffering from this illness may not fully realize what is happening but engage in self-blame. A woman described her experience thus:

'I nursed my mother for about two years. Up every night, but never any difficulty in keeping going. When she died everyone said how sensibly I took it. But six months later it caught up with me – just couldn't stop crying, wanted to shut myself away, felt just so *ill*. I'd had a bottle of brandy in the house for my mother, and I thought, well, it might be a bit of a pick-me-up. I don't think anything happened suddenly, she died eighteen months ago, and, well, I suppose now I'm getting through half a bottle some days, it doesn't really do any good, but to begin with . . .'

The familiar story is often indeed of the woman with untreated depression, who has sought to alleviate her misery with drinking. In the short term alcohol can be potent in giving relief. But it is in fact a bad anti-depressant, which will in many respects make the condition worse, although it may continue to give a transient and superficial relief which encourages its continuing heavy use.

Another quite common underlying psychiatric condition is the severe *anxiety state*; or some form of *situational anxiety*, such as agoraphobia or claustrophobia. Phobic conditions are often treatable, so that diagnosis is of practical importance. Excessive drinking can sometimes be a consequence of loss of psychological control resulting from *organic damage to the brain*. The old person who is suffering from dementia can begin to drink in a dangerous manner, or the young person who for example has sustained a severe head injury in a motor cycle accident may a year later be drinking in a disastrously chaotic fashion. Rarely, excessive drinking may be a complication of mental subnormality.

More unusual mental causes include *schizophrenia*, and particularly that type of illness which has as its end result the person who is psychologically withdrawn, emotionally flattened, and quietly listening to his 'voices', while socially he is homeless, drifting, unable to work, and falling through the systems of social after-care – he just adds drink as one more problem. Occasionally too the person who has periods of abnormal elation (*hypomania*) will drink excessively in the phase of excitement. This is partly perhaps because of the general impairment of judgement and responsibility and sense of free-spending expansiveness that is typical of this disorder, and partly too because the elation may in fact be accompanied by much anxiety, or rather superficially masked depression.

What can, therefore, be concluded from this brief review of the possible relationship between mental illness and drinking is that, although mental illness only makes a relatively small contribution to the genesis of abnormal drinking, the possibilities should be borne in mind. To neglect an underlying mental illness may be harmful, while to treat that illness may be the key to helping with the drinking problem.

The major implications

This chapter can be rounded off by making or reiterating two very simple and definite points.

The first point to be made is one which at this stage must indeed be obvious: *there is a vast amount of available research and observations from many different scientific and clinical disciplines which today bear on the understanding of why people drink harmfully.* This mass of information is a challenge in its own right. It can be left on the library shelves, and quietly ignored while government policies and the daily business of all our dealings go ahead on the basis of uninformed predilections. Alternatively this or that piece of evidence can be taken out of context, accorded dominant importance, and all reservations in interpretation forgotten: price control becomes everything, genetics takes the centre of the stage, early environment is the whole explanation. Different scientific disciplines will each put in their bid and, if the scientists themselves fail to understand each other, it is hardly surprising that the layman is left in a muddle. It is often extraordinarily difficult to establish the satisfactory and sensible follow-through from even a relatively straightforward and delimited piece of research to social action and policies. In this particular instance the complexities and difficulties are such that there is a very live risk of getting lost in a fog. The abolition of the rum ration was recommended in 1834, and implemented in 1968.

The second essential point which must therefore be made is that it really does behove us to ensure that we do not get lost in this fog. The aim must be closely to examine the whole range of evidence and try to take from it *any understandings that offer hope of leverage on the problems concerned.* What we have to identify is very specifically those insights that can practically illuminate the questions of how society can both ameliorate the present appalling rates of alcohol-related damage and treat the people who are suffering.

7

What can be
expected of treatment?

This chapter will not go into the technicalities of treatment methods for alcoholism; such textbook considerations are outside the scope of the Report. However, to understand the role that treatment can play as a part of the country's total response to drinking problems, it is necessary to examine a number of issues. We need, for instance, to look at how the stress that this Report places on the individual's personal responsibility for modifying his own drinking behaviour is compatible with the idea that such behaviour may indeed very much require treatment. The question of how resistances to admitting the existence of a problem are to be overcome is again a matter of more than technical importance. Some basic treatment assumptions and some of the usual treatment methods, as well as some of the current treatment controversies, will be examined briefly. We finally have to look at what treatment can be expected to achieve for the individual, and for society at large.

Personal responsibility

When discussing the implications of the dependence syndrome, we proposed that alcohol dependence was best seen as an *illness*, but in terms of an 'informed notion of illness' which does not deny self-responsibility (p. 56). We have also stressed that, although dependence is indeed a special condition which may greatly impair the individual's control over his drinking once he again starts to drink, the person who is drinking excessively without having contracted dependence may also be having genuine difficulty in controlling his behaviour. These seemingly rather abstract ideas are, in fact, of great practical importance to developing an accurate perspective on the place of treatment.

Some people with drinking problems may be able to deal with their own behaviour without recourse to professional or organized help, and there is good evidence that this is happening in the community all the time. A drinking problem should be a signal for self-questioning and sensible change. Here is an example of a type of story that is not uncommon:

'When I was in the Forces and the war had ended and we were all hanging about with nothing to do, I drank like a fish. Makes me shudder to think about it now – the risks we took driving back to the camp at night. My fiancée broke off our engagement, and I couldn't blame her. When I came back to civvy street, I got in straightaway with a lot of drinkers, and went on knocking the stuff back. I suppose I was about through with spending my gratuity, a lot of money gone, when I said to myself, "This has got to stop". And it meant finding entirely different friends, taking up new leisure interests and chucking in the Rugger Club, and more than anything making up my mind as to what I actually meant to do with my life, rather than just drifting along in a boozy haze. I met another girl I very much liked, and I certainly wasn't going to ruin things again.'

Not everyone's self-determination may have to be harnessed to so serious a problem as that described by the man quoted above, but the practical message is that many people will at some times in their lives have to make small or large modifications in their drinking behaviour, and that the capacity for making such changes often lies well within their powers. They will be much aided by the understanding (and demands) of their families and others around them.

If the simple view were accepted that a drinking problem automatically necessitated professional treatment, then there would be no confusion. But a dilemma inevitably results when it is accepted that some people may be able to do all that is needed by means of their own resources (with society encouraging this view of self-determination), while the message is at the same time given that other people should indeed seek professional help (and should be encouraged to do so without delays which can result in unnecessary further harm). A balance must obviously be struck, and it is not absolutely different in kind from the decisions that people make every day on a host of other medical and social issues – whether for instance a headache is a pain to be endured, dealt with by going to bed early or by taking an analgesic, or a symptom which requires a visit to the doctor.

We are not wishing to discourage appropriate help-seeking, but to encourage everyone's sense of personal responsibility for his or her own drinking: some people who are drinking harmfully, and certainly the person who has contracted the dependence syndrome, may well find it impossible to deal with their situations without special help: with society's present lack of information on the nature of dependence, that person may not even have a clear idea of what he has to deal with, until he can obtain some informed advice.

Overcoming resistances

The common starting point for any constructive changes in behaviour has to be the individual's personal admission and realization that he has a drinking problem; this is equally true whether he is going to remedy the matter by his own efforts, or with professional help, or AA. Unfortunately, it is commonly believed that the 'typical' drinker with a desperately severe problem will adamantly refuse to admit that he has a problem at all, and will stubbornly refuse help despite the manifest damage that he is causing to himself and to his family. Such sad instances on occasion occur, but it is wrong to take the extreme case as typical.

118

In every case, facing up to the facts will be an important personal issue, but it is a matter of *degree*, and we should not assume that extreme denial is always involved.

Of course, the problem of facing worrying facts is not unique to drinking. If someone is frightened or ashamed of his behaviour, he is likely to hide or deny what he is doing; this is an understandable defensive strategy. If he is then simply scolded in an unconstructive fashion, the denial is likely to become more determined. Excessive drinking may often lead to behaviour that is worrying or shaming for the person concerned, and some degree of resistance to seeing the true facts of the situation is therefore hardly surprising.

The ways in which resistance of this sort can be dealt with are several, and overcoming resistance is more often a matter of whittling it away than dealing with it at a stroke.

'Well, I knew he'd got a drinking problem, but for some time he just wouldn't take any notice of what I said. He'd try to avoid the issue, or fly into a rage and put all the blame on me. Went on for a couple of years that way. Wouldn't go to the doctor. I tried leaving A A pamphlets around but he took no more notice of them than of all the bills he didn't pay. I think what finally got through to him was when his brother had a word, and he could see that we were all on his side.'

In addition to the pressures from family or friends, the general climate of attitudes and stock of ideas that society provides with regard to drinking behaviour will also be important, together with more general social attitudes towards deviance, towards the ability to admit problems or to seek help, and so on. If society could more readily accept the idea that drinking problems are common and do not have to be shamefully hidden, then it might indeed be easier for the troubled person to surrender his denials earlier. People who are overweight do not seem to find it too difficult to admit this fact; society's attitudes towards drinking problems need to move in that direction.

If a person with a drinking problem feels himself under severe and unsympathetic attack, he may put up further barriers; but if people around him just say nothing or join in a conspiracy of denial, something even more unhelpful is being done. Both the initiation of change in drinking behaviour and the continued support of the individual who is trying to alter his drinking must therefore be seen as often dependent on interactions with family and friends, rather than lying only with the individual, or only with the professionals.

Readiness to make use of professional help (or to turn to AA) must then depend not only on actual willingness to admit a problem, but also on factual knowledge as to where help may be found, readiness of access, and the attitudes of the professionals when approached. Resistance to recognizing drinking problems or unwillingness to take a constructive and helpful attitude may, on occasion, be problems that reside with the professionals as much as with the drinker himself. The resistances and denials of the doctor who 'never sees drinking problems in *his* practice' are targets for education.

Some basic treatment assumptions

This section will give a description of some basic ideas which underlie treatment of alcoholism. The aim is simply to provide a general understanding of what is *meant* by treatment.

The drinking problem: to be taken seriously but never as the exclusive focus

Anyone who has had experience with the treatment of alcoholism will realize that the drinking problem does not exist in isolation. Likewise, patients sometimes complain that 'drink isn't really the problem'. Such objections rightly remind us that it is a *person* who is coming for help, with an essential sense of being a person with various troubles and perplexities which exist in their own right, and which may predate the excessive drinking, or cause it, or intertwine with it, or exacerbate it. The balance always has to be struck between an insistent awareness of the importance of drinking in the total picture, and the fact that excessive drinking is highly unlikely to be the only problem experienced by the patient. The professional who is going to respond to the alcoholic, besides having special knowledge of drinking problems, has therefore to be capable of a wide perspective: the person required is the social worker with general training, the psychiatrist or physician with a good general knowledge of his subject, the general practitioner, and so on. The philosophy and techniques of Alcoholics Anonymous show, for instance, in well-developed form, this ability to respond to drinking in proper perspective: AA is about coming to terms with alcoholism, but also about coming to terms with oneself, with one's relationships, and with surrounding realities. Too narrow a specialism cannot meet the diversity of physical, social, and psychological problems that relate to alcoholism.

The need for a thorough case assessment

Where there is a drinking problem of any complexity, a two-minute interview is not going to provide the necessary basis of understanding on which to formulate a treatment approach that is personal to the needs of that particular patient and his family. A full assessment will often have to be social, as well as medical and psychological, and may have to involve interviews with the family as well as with the patient.

Gathering a full case history may be important not only for the information that it gives the doctor or social worker or the treatment team, but also in terms of its significance for the patient himself. The business of *sharing* in a review of his present situation and its historical development, the sympathetic invitation to openness, and the conduct of a kind of self-audit, can provide a new self-awareness on which much else can subsequently be built.

Identifying goals

In alcoholism treatment there are special reasons for an emphasis on identifying treatment *goals* (which must again be specific to the particular person and family). Clear goals help to relieve the sense of chaos, of 'everything piling in upon him', and make movement towards recovery possible. Goals may, for instance, relate to physical or psychological health, to the functioning of the marriage, or to such social matters as getting a new job or moving to a better home. Obviously, one important goal must relate to the drinking behaviour – and here the goal may be abstinence (as is usually the case where the dependence syndrome has developed), or the modification of drinking towards a more acceptable pattern. A set of multiple goals has to be developed, rather than a drinking goal only. Goals have to be stepwise and realistic, rather than so ambitiously set from the start as to be defeating. They cannot be imposed, but have to be negotiated with the patient and his family.

The essence of effective treatment often lies in the skill with which such a matter as the setting of goals is handled. A visible target as to what is to be achieved – 'I will take my son to football matches on Saturday afternoons' – restores to the troubled individual some small immediate sense of his own powers and possibilities.

Working towards treatment goals

We have discussed the importance of the patient's self-responsibility, and emphasized that treatment should seek to maximize rather than undermine that individual's sense of responsibility. Treatment must also support, and find alliance with, the helping resources of family and community. Goals can only be approached successfully if the patient is himself working towards their achievement. He may however need some professional guidance as to how best to find the way – and this help may be in the form of relatively brief counselling, or longer-term assistance. On occasion it may be clear that intensive or specialized help is needed if the patient is to be enabled to help himself: at an acute stage he may have to be admitted to hospital so as to be detoxified from alcohol and to receive treatment for severe withdrawal symptoms; his physical health may have to be restored; a severe underlying depressive illness may have to be treated; or a Skid Row alcoholic may have to be found a hostel place and given a way out of a circular and destructive process of degradation.

Goals are thus reached by a variety of methods and often by a variety of forms of co-operation; the patient's own commitment and involvement are essential, the family and the immediate social environment often have an important part to play, while professional help and AA can provide ancillary assistance which must be deployed sensitively and with due regard to the whole person and his family.

Continuing care

Another treatment principle, which is gaining general acceptance, is that patients with the more severe type of drinking problem should be offered continuing contact with a helping agency, at least for the first year of two after commencing treatment. Drinking problems of any severity are never resolved overnight; a patient's greater awareness of his problems often evolves slowly over time and needs for help may similarly evolve, while relapse is inevitably quite a frequent occurrence so that further crisis help may be needed along the way. Some sort of continued watching brief, and the assurance to the patient that someone will continue to be interested in him, is therefore often indicated.

Special treatment methods in outline

In the preceding section some general principles of alcoholism treatment have been discussed. The seemingly rather non-specific influences of such processes as making the assessment, agreeing the goals, and discussing how goals are to be reached may be extremely important therapeutic influences in their own right. But special techniques can on occasion have a part to play, employed within the context of these more general influences. The paragraphs below are not to be taken as listing techniques in order of usefulness: the possible value of any technique must depend on the individual patient.

Psychotherapies

Group psychotherapy has become widely accepted as useful for alcoholics, and is a common basis of treatment régimes in specialized alcoholism units. Marital therapy is being increasingly used for alcoholics' problems. Intensive psychotherapy may on occasion have its place, but is not widely employed for alcoholism. Emphasis is being put on the development of simpler counselling skills.

Alcoholics Anonymous and Alanon

Repeated mention has already been made of the value of Alcoholics Anonymous. It is sound advice to anyone who is developing serious trouble with his drinking to go along to AA meetings and see for himself 'what's in it for him'. Many people have found in AA exactly the help and understanding that they required. Others may take something from AA philosophy and not become regular attenders, but there is never anything to lose in 'having a look'. Alanon deserves similar recognition as an extremely useful resource well worth exploration by anyone closely involved with an alcoholic in the family.

Behaviour therapies

Behaviour therapies, in contrast to psychotherapy, aim to treat the 'problem behaviour' directly, rather than the supposed underlying psychodynamic or personality problems. Over thirty years ago, aversion therapy was the first behavioural treatment method to be developed for alcoholism: the technique attempted to build a simple conditioned aversion to alcohol, by repeatedly giving a patient alcohol by mouth and almost at the same time an injection (apomorphine or emetine) to make him vomit, so that, once the reflex was established, the smell or taste of alcohol would by itself produce nausea. Aversion therapy is for a number of reasons now rather out of fashion, but has had historical importance in stimulating interest in alcoholism treatment (and producing therapeutic optimism). More modern behaviour therapies include simply teaching a patient to be able to say 'no' when offered a drink, teaching him alternative skills with which to meet stress or tension so that he does not have to resort to drink, teaching him to drink more moderately and to judge his own blood alcohol level, or teaching him to put up with slight withdrawal symptoms without taking a morning drink and becoming involved again in a cycle of drinking. Some psychologists today favour the use of a combination of several behaviour techniques tailored to the individual patient's needs – a 'broad spectrum' approach.

Deterrent drugs

Disulfiram (Antabuse) was introduced into clinical practice shortly after World War II. The patient who takes a tablet each day for a few days will, if he then drinks, become nauseated and flushed, and generally feel ill. Disulfiram thus serves as a sort of 'chemical fence' around the drinking. A newer drug, calcium cynamide (Abstem), has also been developed, with similar actions but fewer side-effects, and it is a matter of clinical judgement which drug should be used in particular circumstances. Shock or rarely death can result if a patient drinks heavily when he has taken a full dose of tablets, so this is not a treatment to be given without explanation and close medical supervision. This type of drug treatment has its place, but it is not a panacea, and when these tablets are given it has to be in a context of more general help.

Detoxification

Alcohol withdrawal symptoms have been described in a previous chapter (pp. 43–4): they range from the trivial to the markedly unpleasant or the life threatening (delirium tremens or withdrawal fits). A patient suffering from the dependence syndrome may therefore require immediate and special medical assistance in 'coming off' alcohol. This may often be accomplished by the GP's help or on an out-patient basis, but severe dependence is an indication for hospital admission so that careful observation can be provided, and intensive nursing and medical care are on hand. A variety of drugs may be used to provide pharmacological cover for withdrawal, and specially skilled nursing may be needed for the delirious and agitated patient. Modern methods of care are very successful in treating this acute phase of the problem, and risks to life have been much reduced. Plans which are now developing for 'detoxification centres' should ensure more effective and humane treatment for the severely dependent alcoholic who presents as a drunkenness offender, and who would previously have been detoxified only in the dangerously inappropriate setting of the police cell (see p. 15).

In-patient admission

There is no doubt that some alcoholics will require in-patient care. Admission may be indicated for a variety of physical and psychological complications, for immediate protection of the individual's life, sometimes for the relief of the acutely threatening impact of his behaviour on others, or, on occasion, for detoxification. Whether in-patient care is indicated simply for the treatment of the drinking habit itself (by means, for instance, of group psychotherapy) is to be decided only with reference to the particular patient.

Some treatment controversies

Thus far we have attempted a broad sketch of what treatment is about in terms that might generally be accepted by most professionals who practise in this field. Some note must now be taken of issues on which there would at present be greater diversity of opinion.

Certainly one area of controversy relates to the intensity of the treatment to be offered in given circumstances. Where some experts would advise in-patient care and intensive subsequent after-care, others might advise only a much simpler out-patient approach which would leave more to the patient's own determination. One psychiatrist might advise a particular patient that the best course of action was for him to accept a twelve-week in-patient stay, and intensive after-care, whereas someone else might, after careful assessment, advise only out-patient care, and perhaps only one or two sessions of focussed counselling. Each would agree that there is a place both for in-patient and for out-patient care, and a place for treatments of various grades of intensity: the debate is in essence only on the timing and deployment of the choices, and the initial criteria which might suggest one or the other approach as the first choice. However, if less intensive therapies win wider acceptance, this will have implications for the overall planning of the pattern of treatment services.

The place of specialism is also a subject for debate: the question here is how much of the total potential 'patient load' of people with drinking problems will require specialist referral, as distinct from being adequately helped by general services. It is again necessary to underline that the differences of opinion, though important and with practical implications both for the individual and for the planning of services, are not absolute. It is agreed that there is a place both for the generalist and for the specialist in helping people with drinking problems – the debate is about the ways in which these different aspects of a total service intermesh, support each other's efforts, and together help and support the patient and his family. There is undoubtedly an increasing need to enhance the skills of the non-specialist. This is dictated by the growing realization of the extent and diversity of the drinking problems which afflict the community, and also by the fact that drinking may in major or minor degree be involved in other physical, psychiatric, or social problems, so that the generalist is quite inevitably involved. Many of the presentations do not imply the type of well-developed drinking problem with which the alcoholism specialist has familiarly worked. The problem *range* requires both specialists and non-specialists.

Another matter for lively debate is the drinking goal that can be recommended for the particular patient – a question which has already been touched on (p. 121). Until recently, lifelong abstinence would have been the only goal that could be offered responsibly to a patient who showed evidence of the dependence syndrome. This view has been challenged by those who consider it to be too absolute, and who have produced careful research to show that some patients who have developed dependence may later regain a seemingly confident control over their drinking. The controversy has sometimes been fierce, generating more heat than light. It is best to admit that the 'return to normal drinking' argument is at present not fully resolved, while meanwhile acknowledging that individual judgement as to what constitutes the most responsible and caring advice for a patient remains (after discussion with that patient) the only touchstone.

Additional controversies exist as to which type of special technique is appropriate in what circumstances – whether psychotherapy or behaviour therapy is to be employed, the drug of choice for withdrawal, whether family therapy is indicated, and so on. There can be no doubt that the whole area of alcoholism treatment stands much in need of research which can provide objective answers to these many questions, large and small.

Trends in NHS admission for alcoholism

Table 8 gives information on admissions of alcoholics to NHS hospitals for psychiatric treatment, from 1949 to 1975. The striking rise in such admissions over recent years is clearly seen. These figures take no account of patients who were treated on a purely out-patient basis, nor of patients admitted to general hospitals for treatment of physical complications of alcoholism.

What can be expected of treatment?

So much for a general account of what is meant by treatment, and of the current debates. In the light of what has been said here, what place should be accorded to treatment services within the total strategy of the country's response to drinking problems? Evidence as to the actual *efficacy* of treatment must obviously bear on the answer given to this question, but relevant evidence is in some ways still surprisingly scant. The published research seems to deal almost exclusively with treatment of patients suffering from problems of such degree as to qualify for referral to psychiatric hospitals, where the diagnosis of 'alcoholism' is the starting point for selection and entry to treatment. It may be presumed that such patients are likely to have been suffering from

Table 8 Admissions to mental illness hospitals and units under regional hospital boards and teaching hospitals in England or Wales, where primary or secondary diagnosis was alcoholism or alcoholic psychosis, 1949–75

Year	Primary diagnosis			Secondary diagnosis	Total admissions (Primary or secondary diagnosis)
	Alcoholic psychosis	Alcoholism	Total	Alcoholism only	
1949	214	225	439		
1950					
1951	195	326	512		
1952	204	464	668		
1953	233	542	775		
1954	253	546	799		
1955	393	660	1,053		
1956	551	834	1,385		
1957	531	1,004	1,535		
1958	478	1,117	1,595		
1959	532	1,512	2,044		
1960	609	1,870	2,479		
1961					
1962					
1963					
1964	448	4,975	5,423	1,160	6,583
1965	457	5,317	5,774	1,102	6,876
1966	461	5,627	6,088	1,268	7,356
1967	396	5,8.	6,232	1,409	7,641
1968	353	6,038	6,391	1,425	7,816
1969	360	6,329	6,689	1,376	8,065
1970	917	7,174	8,091	617	8,708
1971	1,353	7,877	9,230	671	9,901
1972	1,514	8,653	10,167	683	10,850
1973	1,714	9,851	11,565	693	12,258
1974	1,750	10,745	12,495	689	11,184
1975	1,657	11,094	12,751	681	13,432
1976	1,784	11,938	13,722	835	14,557

Source: DHSS (personal communication). Since 1970 'depressives not otherwise stated' have been shown in the figures for primary diagnosis whereas previously they were included in the secondary diagnosis figures. This means that when divided into primary and secondary diagnosis the pre-1970 figures are not comparable with post-1970 figures. The totals are of course comparable.

the alcohol dependence syndrome in more or less severe degree. Abstinence has nearly always been the goal which has been advised (at least until the past few years).

Reports from Britain and other countries concur in suggesting that about 60 per cent of patients of this type will show worthwhile or substantial improvement at the end of a twelve-month follow-up, although nearly always less than half of that 60 per cent will have achieved complete or nearly complete abstinence for the full twelve months. Multiple measures of change in status will often be employed, which will include not only changes in drinking behaviour, but work status, criminal behaviour, marital adjustment, physical health, and various psychological measures. Improvement in the drinking is usually, but not always, related to improvement in these other measures. Outcome after one year is generally thought to be a fair pointer to subsequent prognosis; although some patients will certainly show a later relapse (either transiently or more disastrously), others may begin to show significant improvement only after a longer struggle.

However, there are some necessary caveats as regards the full significance to be accorded the sort of figures just quoted. First, it has to be noted that about 40 per cent of patients in general appear to derive little benefit from the best endeavours of the treatment services (at least over the usual period of observation). With such a potentially devastating condition as alcoholism a 60 per cent success rate is cause for optimism, but the fact that treatment fails to benefit another significant proportion of patients cannot be left out of the reckoning. It must also be noted that the sort of success rate that we are quoting here is the type of result that is generally reported from specialized units which have a fairly rigorous process of selection. Indeed, even more rigorous screening, accepting for treatment only patients with the most favourable outlook, will result in a success rate considerably above the one that we have given. Even levels of around 60 per cent success are, however, usually based on selection of patients who are to a considerable extent 'motivated for treatment', and it is not unusual for patients with 'severe personality disorder' to be rejected at the initial screening, for patients with severe physical damage (and particularly brain damage) to be selected out as 'too deteriorated', while homeless alcoholics are also often excluded. The overall impact of the selection process may be such as to produce, as the basis for the research report, a group of patients biased towards a personality profile and degree of social stability which are atypical of the larger reality. Good results can to an extent be obtained by stacking the cards, and results from centres where case selection has been less rigorous do not look so cheerful – favourable outcome may then be obtained with only 20 per cent to 30 per cent of subjects. This is not to suggest that the often excellent results obtained from specialized treatment centres should be considered in any way spurious, or that they should be discounted. They speak, however, only of the type of result which can be expected with a segment of the total potential case load.

Still focussing only on the patient with the dependence syndrome or with the more serious type of drinking problem, we then have to pursue a little further the question of what percentage of all such persons in the community are in practice making contact with helping agencies. Ideally, the way to answer this question would be to conduct a survey which would identify and enumerate all individuals in a given community who have serious drinking problems, and then to determine what proportion of these patients were in contact with helping agencies. Such research is difficult and expensive, and has seldom been attempted, but a limited project bearing on this question was conducted in Camberwell in 1966. It revealed that only 11 per cent to 22 per cent of people with a serious drinking problem had been in contact with an appropriate agency during the previous year.

Taking another set of figures, DHSS data suggest that there are currently about 13,500 admissions annually to NHS hospitals in England and Wales for treatment of alcoholism (see *Table 8*); this has to be put against estimates of the total national prevalence of alcoholism which range between 300,000 and 500,000. The contribution of non-specialist agencies, particularly the general practitioner, out-patient care, private practice, voluntary agencies, and Alcoholics Anonymous, would have to be added to these DHSS in-patient admission figures. But by any reckoning it does appear that the treatment system (even defined in the broadest sense), is at present reaching only a rather small proportion of people who stand in need.

One response to this type of calculation, which sets out the probable ratio between the size of the problem population and the extent of treatment actually delivered, would be to argue that the figures clearly show the need to increase the treatment facilities and to run a more active campaign to bring people into treatment. Such a policy might be expected to bring benefits, but it also seems possible that a law of diminishing returns might begin to operate: there may be a limit to the proportion of those with serious drinking problems who are willing to enrol as 'patients' or are able to benefit from the available treatments. There will also be a limit to the country's willingness and capacity to allocate resources to the costs of treating this problem, since it is only one among the many demands on the budget and manpower of the NHS. Treatment certainly has a vital, continuing, and evolving place within the total strategy of the country's response to drinking problems, but the facts suggest that it would be a false expectation to hope that treatment services could be so developed that the majority of people with serious drinking problems could ever be brought into treatment and effectively treated.

So far the discussion has centred on the type of person who is sufficiently badly affected by his drinking to become a patient in a psychiatric hospital or special alcoholism unit, or to figure in the DHSS 'alcoholism' statistics, or to be identified in a community survey as having a serious drinking problem. As has already been stated, the reason for taking this initial focus is that the great bulk of the research data deals only with this type of case. What would happen if treatment were offered to, for example, the man or woman who is not alcohol dependent and not a continuous drinker, but who has, say, on a particular occasion, driven when intoxicated, or who is occasionally abusive or violent in the home when drunk, or who just sometimes spends too much of the week's wages on drink – this is a very different question. For a whole range of drinking behaviours – resulting in minor or occasionally very major adverse consequences – it is not obvious that 'treatment', in any conventional sense, is appropriate. Quite often the damage will have been done before the person is likely to have come to the notice of anyone but his family and friends – we are thinking here of the case of drunken driving, the home accident, the drunken fall on the pavement on Saturday night, the drunken brawl and the unpremeditated assault, and so on. What society is to prescribe for a wide range of problems which may be engendered by non-dependent drinking becomes an important question once it is realized that the sum of the damage which the country experiences as a result of abnormal drinking extends far beyond the limits set by the dependent drinker, and of the traditional focus of medical and psychiatric concern. On present evidence there would be no grounds at all for supposing that the bulk of this problem could be dealt with by bringing a whole new segment of the population into formal treatment. Even supposing that, for instance, all 63,000 people charged with drunk driving each year wanted to enter treatment, there is insufficient evidence that we would know how to treat them; nor could resources be found to meet such a demand. Again, there has to be a sense of perspective: treatment will help some drunken drivers, and it is urgent to identify those with serious drinking problems for whom there would be benefit from treatment, but society simply cannot hope to meet anything approaching the major segment of the drunk driving problem, or many other similar problems, with a cry for 'more treatment'.

In summary, we believe the facts suggest that two equally essential conclusions should be drawn as to what society may expect of treatment. The first conclusion is that treatment very often has something vitally important to offer: the person who is worried about his drinking should know that if he cannot deal with things himself it is greatly in his interests to seek professional advice or go to AA, and to do so early. Treatment services need to be strengthened to allow this. But the second conclusion (which in no way contradicts the first) is that, in terms of national strategies, the contribution that treatment can be expected to make is definitely limited. In the final chapter we shall consider how these appraisals bear on recommendations for future national strategies, both for treatment and for the prevention of drinking problems.

8

A better response

That a better response by society to its drinking problems is needed should not be in doubt. At this point it is worthwhile once more to state squarely what is fundamentally at stake. Lives are being ruined on a large scale by the abuse of alcohol. It is easy to become so dulled by the toll of casualties as not to notice the magnitude of the suffering. We cease to look behind the statistics, and forget that each death from cirrhosis represents the end of a very personal tragedy, and that the human wreck dozing with his meths bottle on the park bench is someone's son, or husband, or father. We ignore these visible manifestations of society's inability to cope with the alcohol problem only at our long-term peril. In seventeen out of eighteen major industrialized countries alcohol consumption has risen steadily since the last war, and alcohol-related disabilities are on the increase in most parts of the world. We may try to comfort ourselves with the knowledge that there are countries with more serious problems than Britain, but the sort of data that this Report has presented on our own national trends should quickly dispel any sense of self-satisfaction. Some of the key facts are worth recapitulating. In England and Wales consumption of wine has almost doubled since 1969, and that of spirits has exactly doubled. The annual figure for drunkenness arrests rose from 47,717 to 103,203 between 1950 and 1974. The number of people admitted to mental hospital with a diagnosis of alcoholism or alcohol psychosis has been climbing at a rate of about 10 per cent each year – from 439 in 1949 to 13,432 in 1975. While the total number of drivers involved in all accidents rose at a rate of 2·3 per cent annually between 1968 and 1973, the proportion of these accidents in which a positive breath test was obtained rose by 27 per cent. Again it is necessary to look beyond the statistics to the personal realities of suffering, wasted life, and family misery. Very clearly, present actions are not only failing to decrease the occurrence of alcohol-related damage, but are failing even to contain their increase.

In this final chapter a number of recommendations will be made. These suggestions will deal as much with ways of looking at problems as with concrete actions: the two aspects are equally vital. To make recommendations is of course to risk being attacked for being too vague, too assured, or plain wrong-headed. These risks are taken in the belief that a report of this nature must reach conclusions rather than dodge every issue as being too difficult, insufficiently researched, or somebody else's business: the crucial issues in alcoholism are too often evaded. It is not however presumed that these recommendations constitute some sort of grand or grandiose blueprint: they are meant as basis for debate.

Prevention

The need for a new emphasis on prevention

We believe that prevention is receiving pitifully inadequate attention. Alcoholism is in this regard no exception to the general pattern of health expenditure in this country, and indeed most other parts of the world. Gigantic and increasing sums are being spent on treatment of illness, while prevention of ill-health is a notion more honoured in theory than in practice. About £5,000 million are now spent annually in Britain on the National Health Service, and of this huge sum roughly £88 million is estimated as being devoted to preventive work. *In 1975 the total spent on*

*advertising alcoholic drinks was about £27 million: the total budget
allocated to the Health Education Council for the whole range of its
activities on every health topic was £1½ million.*

We make the recommendation that:

* Health policies on alcoholism should generally give much
  greater attention to prevention than has previously been the
  case.

The recommendations which we will make on prevention are in
line with views expressed in the report of the Expenditure Committee of the House of Commons, and also with those of the
Report on Prevention of the DHSS Advisory Committee on Alcoholism. We wish to support the suggestions of those two committees, but believe that matters now have to be taken further, as
our own recommendations will show.

The need for visible goals

It is more emotionally satisfying and often more engaging of
public sympathies and national energies when an attack can be
made on a social problem with the battle cry that, if only we attack with sufficient vigour and resolve, the problem can absolutely be rooted out. Issues such as the slave traffic, or smallpox,
could engender an enormous campaigning commitment, both
nationally and internationally. What has to be faced with alcoholism is that society has no intention or prospect of *eliminating*
the problem. In the absence of any such clear and absolute aim
there is inevitable confusion as to the policy goals that will actually be pursued. Society is not going to eliminate alcoholism, for
the plain reason that it has no intention of eliminating the use of
alcohol. The evidence presented in Chapter 6 must be taken as
firmly supporting the view that the level and manner in which a
country uses alcohol will be related to the scale of the damage
which alcohol will inflict on that country. It is easily forgotten
that prohibition was once mooted in this country, but today it
would be politically inconceivable to inflict that degree of control on the individual pursuit of pleasure, and would imply a degree of paternalism contrary to the spirit of the times. If the

American prohibition experiment is relevant, it also seems likely that an attempt to ban alcohol in a society which widely desires this substance would lead to a criminally organized black market. Not only is alcohol a source of pleasure which our society would be unwilling to surrender, but it is also a source of profit, employment, and tax revenue on a huge scale. In 1975 a total of 64,200 people were employed in brewing and malting in England and Wales, and 10,300 persons in other drink industries. As long ago as 1969, the Brewers' Society estimated that the brewing industry in the UK had a capital investment of £1,700 millions (not far short of the total capital investment in the manufacture of food-stuffs). Revenue to the Government from Customs and Excise duty and VAT on alcohol now runs at well over £2,000 million each year. No wonder there is conflict over the response to drinking problems.

What level of casualty is then to be taken as *acceptable*? This is a practical question of much human interest which must be brought more into the open. Is the country willing to say that on this or that index the climb has been intolerable, that it must be made to reverse the trend? It is the 'targetlessness' of society's present policies on alcohol problems that guarantees failure. One remedy would be to propose that certain definite goals be set up and publicly acknowledged by the Government. When intentions have been publicly and concretely stated, progress can be effectively monitored.

As a simple set of first-level goals there should be commitment to:

* Preventing the national *per capita* alcohol consumption from rising beyond the present level.
* Preventing a further rise in any of the available indices of alcohol-related harm – with cirrhosis deathrate perhaps providing a particularly useful index.

It might further be suggested that, as a minimal second-stage set of goals, some agreement should be reached as to the level to which alcohol consumption and indices of harm (including cirrhosis deathrate) should be *brought down* over the next decade. We cannot ourselves propose definite targets at this stage, acknowledging that such targets can only be set on the basis of consultation and public debate, informed by a knowledge of the facts. For instance, it might be accepted that the population did not feel itself grossly deprived of drinking opportunities ten years ago, and it might be an agreed goal to bring the national alcohol consumption back to that previous level. Any chosen goal is arbitrary: the criteria must certainly include the element of political feasibility.

Prevention and government policy

Alcoholism is in many ways a test case for the ability of the administrative structure to tackle a complex problem which crosses orthodox boundaries. There exists a DHSS Committee on Alcoholism (see p. 21) which has wide representation; there was a Home Office Committee on the Drunkenness Offender; the Department of the Environment produced a report on drunk driving; the Home Office set up a Committee on Liquor Licensing; taxation is a matter for the Chancellor; education in schools is within the purview of the Department of Education and Science. It would be difficult to find any department which is not in some way involved with questions related to alcohol or alcoholism. Only on the basis of concerted planning is it possible to envisage society dealing effectively with a problem of these protean manifestations, and able continually to evolve policies that can respond to changing conditions and knowledge. Any recommendations in this Report must be sensitive to the working methods of others. With that proviso we would recommend that:

* Urgent attention should be given to means of effecting improvement in consultation and working co-operation between different departments of government so as to ensure an integrated, effective, and evolving response to the country's drinking problems and their interrelatedness.

The further recommendations on prevention policies we now proceed to make stem directly from the discussion of causes of harmful drinking in Chapter 6. We recommend:

* Public revenue policies of government should be intentionally employed in the interest of health, so as to ensure that *per capita* alcohol consumption does not increase beyond the present level, and is by stages brought back to an agreed lower level.

* There should be no further relaxation in the broad range of licensing provisions.

Besides these measures which seek to make more rational and pronounced use of economic and legislative control over alcoholism and drinking we also recommend further investment in preventive approaches through change in cultural attitudes which influence drinking. Health education in this area experiences many problems and facile attempts to influence deeply-held cultural beliefs cannot be expected to succeed. This field of endeavour is much in need of imaginative ideas, emphasis on concrete behaviours rather than generalities, and studies which allow reliable measurement of outcome. We therefore recommend:

* There should be a greatly enhanced government commitment towards public education and persuasion (and relevant research), so as to bring about a reduction in drinking problems.

It may also be useful to make some preliminary recommendations as to the general content of the educational messages:

* Education on alcoholism directed to the general public should:

(a) Attempt continuously to provide the knowledge needed *to inform public debate* so that acceptance may be won for the need for a broad range of preventive measures. The fact that alcohol is a *drug* should be made widely known, the meaning and implications of *dependence*, the nature and extent of *disabilities*, the dangers of *harm done to others*, and the *causes of harmful drinking*. In particular, the *relationship between national* per capita *consumption and the extent of the country's drinking problems* should be brought to public attention.

(b) Inform the community that the use of alcohol in the attempt to relieve unpleasant feelings when people are apprehensive, dejected, depressed, lonely, or bored, carries considerable risks.

(c) Encourage *public disapproval of intoxication*, and foster the attitudes that it is bad manners to get drunk (rather than that it is bad manners to comment on drunkenness).

(d) Give *clear information as to what constitutes safe or dangerous levels of drinking*. We would suggest that an intake of four pints of beer a day, four doubles of spirits, or one standard-sized bottle of wine constitute reasonable guidelines for the upper limit of drinking. It is unwise to make a habit of drinking even at these levels, and anyone driving a vehicle should not drink at all before driving.

Some comment is needed on the expected pay-off from each of these recommendations for a health education agenda. The simple provision of information cannot be expected by itself to influence drinking behaviour or related problems, but it is relevant to building the climate of informed opinion on which so much else may depend. This information is as much for administrators, Members of Parliament, and the professions as for the population at large. Neither can messages on the use of alcohol as a drug, or on disapprobation of intoxication, be expected to have a direct or immediate influence on attitudes which are culturally ingrained, but they may serve to inform the general debate, get discussion going, and support other efforts. The message given by the individual doctor or teacher, the position taken by a neighbour, the way in which the next television play is presented or the next novel is written, and the attitudes of other immediate and intimate educators or agents of change may thus be influenced or given support.

As for the proposal regarding what constitutes a safe level of drinking, different people react differently to the same dose of any drug, and such additional factors as body weight, for instance, must of course influence the response to a given dose. The way in which any total daily quantity is spaced out during the day will influence its effects. But without some statement on this issue of the acceptable amount to drink a question which many people repeatedly and legitimately ask goes unanswered. The levels given here may be taken as provisional and as a subject for debate. They accord with present scientific findings on relationships between drinking levels and risks of damage, but it should be admitted that information on these relationships is not yet complete. The general principle that quantity drunk is a matter of health concern does need, however, to be established. Too often the educational message has only been in terms of the symptoms of dependence or disability, or the motivations for drinking, rather than the actual fact of alcohol intake.

The enormous amount of money being spent on liquor advertising has already been noted. It is difficult to determine whether this weight of advertising merely encourages brand-switching, or encourages drinking itself. Stripped of conventional reticence, what must now be accepted is that this money is being spent on advertising a psycho-active and potentially addictive drug. It would be surprising if those thousands of attractive hoardings did not in some way augment pressures. The pervasive images which associate glamour and good times with drinking could be viewed as propaganda for the notion that alcohol is indispensable to the realization of some of our most cherished fantasies. We are however aware of the dangers of too much State interference based on too little evidence, and would here make a provisional recommendation:

* The Government should commission research into the impact of liquor advertising, and should be willing to curtail such advertising if the evidence warrants this.

The voluntary *Code of Advertising Practice* has a special section on alcohol, but advertisers seem not infrequently to put a lax interpretation on its provisions.

An earlier recommendation was that one of the two prime and publicly stated goals should be to hold steady (and then reduce) the cirrhosis deathrate (p. 137). Cirrhosis was chosen not so much because of the importance of the condition in its own right, but because scientific evidence points to its value as a general indication of the level of alcohol-related disabilities. Cirrhosis deathrate is not however an entirely satisfactory indicator of trends in the whole range of physical, mental, and social disabilities related to excessive use of alcohol, and to monitor the efficacy of preventive policies there should be sustained effort to improve the wider information base. What is being suggested here are methods for ensuring that the 'necessary intelligence' is continuously available for the monitoring of public health and evaluating the success of preventive efforts. This should not be misread as an excuse for any procrastination in implementing preventive policies.

* Government should take responsibility for examining the reliability of present indices of alcohol consumption and alcohol-related disabilities, their improvement, and their collation, and should commission whatever additional research is necessary for the continued monitoring of preventive policies, either directly or through university departments.

Some of the recommendations that are made here concerning the Government's role in prevention may be regarded as a potential threat to the interests and livelihood of those who have invested their capital in the production of alcohol, or whose livelihood depends on its manufacture, distribution, sale, or advertising. Figures have been given which underline the size of these interests (p. 137), and it would be inequitable if they were treated in cavalier fashion. The liquor industry has already shown concern with alcohol abuse and contributed to research and education. This Report is concerned with furtherance of health, but its recommendations must also take other important and legitimate interests into account.

* The possible impact that health-directed policies on alcoholism may have on the livelihood of any section of the community should be borne in mind, those interests should be consulted, and efforts should be made to devise strategies that protect these interests.

The table we gave on page 95 showed increased alcohol consumption in Britain, in the context of a general international trend. The degree of international co-operation which has existed for over half a century as regards trade and traffic in drugs and related monitoring and exchange of information (with full

British participation) is in contrast to the nearly non-existent concern with international trade in alcohol. In 1975, however, the World Health Assembly adopted a resolution addressed to member states and to the Director General of the WHO, calling for the development of monitoring systems on alcohol consumption and on other relevant data needed for public health policies on an international scale. The Council of Europe has recently taken some initiative on health aspects of drinking, and the International Council on Alcoholism and Addictions is a voluntary organization which has been actively fostering international collaboration for many years. A different type of international influence may, though, be experienced over the next decade in Britain as a result of EEC trade agreements. We therefore recommend that:

* This country should strongly support initiatives for international co-operation in the study of drinking problems, and at the same time should press for a priority consideration of *health* and *social implications* relating to import and export of alcohol rather than accepting the dominance of the economic interest.

Prevention at community and personal level

All levels of prevention interreact with one another: government strategies on control or pricing, the methods of health education, and the actions taken by the community. Special effort must be made to support prevention at the community level, and inherent in the message of education should be the insistence that much of the responsibility lies squarely with the community.

Prevention at community and personal level is best designed in detail by the people immediately concerned. Here are some preliminary recommendations:

* Every industrial or commercial undertaking should review the extent to which its employees are under pressure to drink, and then devise means for lessening this pressure. This is especially important where drinking may affect safety or responsible decisions.
* Special preventive programmes should be set up for high-risk

143

trades or professions, in collaboration with trade unions or appropriate professional organizations.

* A review should be made in every community of the extent to which leisure activities are available (particularly for the young) that do not engender pressures to drink. Appropriate action should be taken to increase the range of such activities.

* Those responsible for organizing official receptions and similar public functions would be wise to serve alcohol only in small quantities, and non-alcoholic drinks should always be available.

* Those who entertain in their own homes should realize that serving alcohol is a responsibility which cannot be treated casually. The amount of alcohol provided for each person should certainly not be in excess of the levels for daily intake mentioned previously (p. 140). Non-alcoholic drinks should always be available.

* Ordinary members of the community should not ignore the person who is drinking excessively but should show the same active concern as they would towards any other potentially dangerous behaviour.

* Every person should accept responsibility for his own personal prevention programme in terms of not exceeding the daily intake level that has been suggested, and if he is exceeding this level he should review the reasons and circumstances, and cut down on his drinking. Exactly the same cautions as previously stated have to be borne in mind when interpreting any specification of an upper limit.

These recommendations only point to a few examples of the ways in which there might be community involvement. Some of the recommendations deal with small issues (the serving of alcohol at a mayor's reception for instance), and it might be objected that such recommendations are pontificating or rather trivial and of merely nuisance value. But only the sum of a great many small or symbolic actions within the community will slowly alter attitudes that have to be altered.

Treatment

A basic assumption

To give treatment its proper context within an awareness of what the individual may be able to accomplish by himself, and of what society's ordinary and informal processes may be expected to accomplish, we recommend the following basic assumption on the place of treatment:

* Skilled help should be available to the person with a drinking problem and in many instances people should be persuaded to seek advice earlier than is at present happening. At the same time the capacity of the individual with a drinking problem to help himself and modify his own behaviour needs to be much more heavily emphasized, as does the importance of the family and the wider society in responding to an individual's excessive drinking in a helpful way.

This recommendation derives from the discussion of the issue of personal responsibility in Chapter 7 (pp. 116–18).

The planning of treatment services

Over the last two decades much has been learnt about treatment and the organization of treatment, and this constitutes the essential basis of experience on which the future of treatment has to build. Whatever the imperfections in the coverage which services have offered, a great many people have found their way to treatment, and many have been helped. But it can nonetheless be argued that despite all the dedicated effort, and the many successes, society has largely been *pretending* to mount a treatment response to alcoholism. A great deal of pretence has got to be swept away before we can appreciate the limited, but vital place which treatment of drinking problems should be accorded. The helping professions must not be put into a position of conniving with a false view of their role and powers. This or that type of scheme comes into official favour while the true significance of any likely impact is not closely questioned before the investment is made. An inflated belief in what treatment can achieve may be a block to true progress if it breeds complacency or leads to neglect of prevention.

The first recommendation which we make has relevance to the broad strategy of planning treatment services:

* The evolution of national policies on treatment services for alcoholism should be designed in terms of critical appraisal of (a) the efficacy of any particular treatment, (b) the appropriateness of the scale upon which that kind of treatment can be introduced within available resources, and (c) the proportion of people with drinking problems who are likely to avail themselves of the help of that treatment.

To some extent this is to commend what is no more than the obvious and generally accepted basis of service planning, but in so far as that is the case no harm is done. Although recent history provides instances of policies being evolved on just this type of basis (e.g. the piloting of detoxification centres), it would on the other hand not be at all difficult to cite aspects of service planning which have not followed these simple rules (the expansion of hostel places, for example). Rather than long periods of inaction being followed by a hurried launching of new schemes with 'no time for research' it would be better if services were evolved and researched as elements of a more continual and related process.

In line with previous discussion of excessive drinking as part of a wider network of causes which contribute to the origins and presentation of a 'drinking' problem (p. 58), the recommendations can then be made that:

* Treatment of alcohol-related disabilities should frequently be left within the province of non-specialized agencies.
* There is a continued place for specialized centres, both for treatment of some patients and for support and training of the generalist who will be dealing with drinking problems.

These recommendations do not enter into details of service planning, but are intended to support the idea that there is room both for the generalist (general practitioner, social worker, nurse, voluntary worker, for instance) and for specialism (special NHS units, specialized voluntary organizations, and so on). What is needed is a continuing exploration of the role of particular agencies and their interrelationship, with an emphasis on the further development of relevant skills among less specialized workers. These recommendations are, we believe, in line with current DHSS thinking and the advice of the DHSS Advisory Committee on Alcoholism.

Professional education

The ability of any profession to make its contribution to the treatment of drinking problems must then depend both on willingness to participate and on trained skills. We would therefore propose that:

* Each relevant caring profession should systematically examine the role which its members can play in the treatment of drinking problems, should review the present adequacy of training to meet these responsibilities, and in the light of such considerations formulate and institute appropriate training.

This last recommendation is purposely made in general terms. It would be wrong for a report coming from one particular professional body to make detailed proposals as to how any other profession – social workers, clinical psychologists, nurses, pastoral counsellors, to name only a few – should go about the task of review. Some organizations have indeed in recent years already made definite moves on professional education in the field of alcoholism. But the recommendation being made here need not be seen as in any way less strongly intended because it takes account of the different situations of different professions – there is undoubtedly a very general need for professions to review the way in which they are dealing with drinking problems.

Research

A strong emphasis on the need for research is implicit in much of what has already been written in this Report. Rather than now setting out a 'shopping list' of research topics, we shall make one general recommendation.

This relates to the planning and integration of research. The degree to which research should be centrally planned or alternatively left to the interests of particular individuals and research centres is of course a question that goes wider than alcoholism research. But with alcohol and alcoholism there are a number of considerations that specially support the desirability of planning. As regards social investigations, there is often a need for *repeated surveys* (repeated monitoring of national drinking patterns, for instance), or for *long-term follow-up* of particular groups (people with different types of drinking problem or different drinking patterns, the children of alcoholics, and so on). There is also often *a need to anticipate events*: a change in licensing provision or an abrupt change in pricing should be proceeded as well as followed by research. There is indeed a general need for *research and social policy to be integrated*, whether this is in relation to any of the prevention strategies that have been discussed, or in relation to the design of treatment services and the development of treatment.

Interdisciplinary research is needed of a type which the ordinary structure of university departments does not necessarily encourage. The general question of *the need to set priorities* applies urgently to alcoholism research because resources are as usual inevitably limited but the array of medico-social problems are of enormous and pressing seriousness. The *exchange of scientific information*, even on such an obvious topic as who is doing what research, the *collation of existing data*, and the *training of research workers* are also matters that should fall within an integrated plan.

The need for planning should here be taken very seriously in that it provides a test case for the scientific policy-making of this country. We recommend that:

* Government departments, the Medical Research Council, and the Social Research Council (with appropriate external scientific representation) should set up the mechanism for an integrated planning of national policies on alcohol and alcoholism research, and for definite periodic up-dating of the plan.

Into the future

Society has chosen to co-exist with a potentially dangerous and addictive drug. It must be accepted by society that responsibility lies with it for dealing with the problems that arise, and for as best as possible averting the occurrence of those problems. The helping professions are part of society and their role and the powers and limitations of what they can offer have to be understood by society. These professions need the community's support.

Society has in many ways tried to have its pleasure, deny its responsibilities, and hand the problem over to the courts or the caring agencies. We believe that an undoubted message for the future is that prevention has to be strengthened, and that this will inevitably mean all of us drinking somewhat less. We cannot pretend to be concerned while complaining that any diminution of our pleasures or profits is too great a price.

Society also needs to deal with its fantasies and its prejudices. People with drinking problems are very much 'of us' – they are not to be put aside as a strange, abhorrent, and disgraced minority. Future action on these problems requires understanding of their pervasiveness in our society and, in every sense, their pain. The problems are complex, and we are a long way from being able to produce any easy and final solution. Society should, though, be appalled by the present state of affairs and entirely unwilling to witness continued loss and suffering of this unnecessary order.

Bibliography

One way of dealing with a bibliography for this Report would have been to provide full references to support every statement made, as would be the usual academic practice. Rather than adopt that academic style, we shall give a relatively brief bibliography of key references, purposely designed to be of practical use to the sort of wide readership we have in mind.

(1) General

Glatt, M. M. (1975) *Alcoholism – A Social Disease*. London: Teach Yourself Books.

Hawker, A. (ed.) (1976) *Alcohol Use and Abuse*. London: Medical Council on Alcoholism.

Kessel, N. and Walton, H. (1965) *Alcoholism*. Harmondsworth: Penguin.

Zacune, J. and Hensman, C. (1971) *Drugs, Alcohol and Tobacco in Britain*. London: Heinemann Medical.

(2) Models, definitions, and the dependence syndrome

Jellinek, E. M. (1960) *The Disease Concept of Alcoholism*. New Brunswick, NJ: Hillhouse Press. (A classic work by the founder of modern alcoholism studies.)

World Health Organization (1977) *Alcohol-Related Disabilities* (Offset Publication No. 32). Geneva: WHO. (Basic exposition of the idea of the dependence syndrome together with other reviews and a lexicon of terms.)

(3) Alcohol as a drug

Ritchie, J. M. (1975) The Aliphatic Alcohols. In, L. S. Goodman and A. Gilman (ed.) *The Pharmacological Basis of Therapeutics* (5th ed.). New York: Macmillan. (Short review chapter in standard American textbook.)

Wallgren, H. and Barry, H. (1970) *Actions of Alcohol: Volume 1 – Biochemical, Physiological and Psychological Aspects*. Amsterdam: Elsevier Publishing. (Technical review.)

(4) Alcohol-related disabilities

Disabilities in general

Hore, B. (1976) *Alcohol Dependence*. London: Butterworths. (Short standard textbook dealing with disabilities among many other topics.)

US Department of Health, Education and Welfare (1974) *Alcohol and Health: New Knowledge*. Washington: DHEW. (Major reviews on several health topics.)

Drunkenness offenders

Cook, T. (1975) *Vagrant Alcoholics*. London: Routledge and Kegan Paul. (Extensive review, and the development of the Alcoholics Recovery Project.)

Home Office (1971) *Habitual Drunken Offenders*. London: HMSO. (Report of Home Office Working Party.)

Drunk driving

Department of the Environment (1976) *Drinking and Driving*. London: HMSO. (Report of the Blennerhassett Committee.)

Much information on alcohol-related disabilities will also be found in books listed as (1) **General**.

(5) Causes of alcoholism, and prevention

Sociology of drinking and alcoholism

Davies, J. and Stacey, B. (1972) *Teenagers and Alcohol*. London: HMSO. (Glasgow study by Jahoda and Cramond continued.)

Jahoda, G. and Cramond, J. (1972) *Children and Alcohol*. London: HMSO. (Developmental study in Glasgow.)

MacAndrew, C. and Edgerton, R. B. (1970) *Drunken Comportment: A Social Explanation*. London: Nelson. (Synthesis of anthropological findings.)

McCord, W. and McCord, J. (1960) *Origins of Alcoholism*. London: Tavistock. (Extensive US research report on childhood background of alcoholics.)

Mass Observation (1943) *The Pub and the People: A Worktown Study*. London: Gollancz. (An English classic.)

Moss, M. C. and Davies, E. B. (1967) *A Survey of Alcoholism in an English County*. London: Geigy. (Epidemiological study in Cambridgeshire.)

Robinson, D. (1976) *From Drinking to Alcoholism: A Sociological Commentary*. London: Wiley. (A review, and a report on a recent study.)

Influence of price and 'formal controls' on alcoholism rates

Bruun, K. *et al.* (1975) *Alcohol Control Policies in Public Health Perpsective*. Helsinki: Finnish Foundation for Alcohol Studies. (Review of the international evidence.)

Home Office (1972) *Report of the Departmental Committee on Liquor Licensing*. London: HMSO. (Erroll Report.)

Robinson, D. *et al.* (1973) *Where Erroll went wrong on Liquor Licensing*. London: Camberwell Council on Alcoholism. (Critique.)

Scottish Home and Health Department (1974) *Report of the Departmental Commiittee on Scottish Licensing Law*. Edinburgh: HMSO. (Clayson Report.)

Genetics

Goodwin, D. (1976) *Is Alcoholism Hereditary?* New York: Oxford University Press.

Advisory Committee on Alcoholism (1977) *Report on Prevention.* London: DHSS and the Welsh Office.

Parliamentary Expenditure Committee (1977) *First Report from the Expenditure Committee, Session 1976–77: Preventive Medicine.* London: HMSO.

(6) Treatment

General

Armor, D. J., Polich, J. M., and Stambul, H. B. (1976) *Alcoholism and Treatment.* Santa Monica, Calif.: Rand Corporation. (Major review and American research report.)

Larkin, E. J. (1974) *The Treatment of Alcoholism.* Toronto: Addiction Research Foundation. (Short general account of theory, practice, and treatment evaluation.)

Miller, P. M. (1976) *Behavioural Treatment of Alcoholism.* Oxford: Pergamon.

Ritson, B. and Hassall, C. (1970) *The Management of Alcoholism.* Edinburgh: Livingstone. (The work of special units.)

Steiner, C. (1971) *Games Alcoholics Play.* New York: Grove Press. (Psychotherapy.)

Wilkins, R. H. (1974) *The Hidden Alcoholic in General Practice.* London: Elek Science. (Detection and the overcoming of resistance: research study.)

Treatment is also extensively discussed in books in the **General** list (1), and in Hore, B. (1976) under **Alcohol-related disabilities** (4).

Planning of treatment services

Cartwright, A. K. J., Shaw, S. J., and Spratley, T. A. (1975) *Designing a Comprehensive Community Response to Problems of Alcohol Abuse.* Mimeograph. London: Maudsley Alcohol Pilot Project. (A review and report of research in a London borough.)

Department of Health and Social Security (1975) *Better Services for the Mentally Ill.* London: HMSO. (Chapter gives DHSS thinking on alcoholism services.)

Alcoholics Anonymous (1939) *Alcoholics Anonymous: 'The Big Book'*. New York: Alcoholics Anonymous World Services, Inc.
Robinson, D. and Henry, S. (1977) *Self-Help and Health*. London: Martin Robertson. (Discussion of A A within context of general analysis of self-help organizations.)

Additional information and pamphlets may be obtained from local Secretaries, or from:

Al-Anon, 61 Great Dover Street, London, SE1 4YF
Alcoholics Anonymous, 11, Redcliffe Gardens, London, SW10

(7) International context

Finnish Foundation for Alcohol Studies (1977) *International Statistics on Alcoholic Beverages*. Helsinki: Finnish Foundation for Alcohol Studies. (Production, trade and consumption for 177 countries, 1950–72.)
Moser, J. (1974) *Problems and Programmes Related to Alcohol and Drug Dependence in 33 Countries* (Offset Publication No. 6). Geneva: WHO.

(8) History

Glatt, M. M. (1971) *Abuse of Alcohol – A Historical Perspective*. In, J. Zacune and C. Hensman, *Drugs, Alcohol and Tobacco in Britain*. London: Heinemann Medical.
Harrison, B. (1971) *Drink and the Victorians*. London: Faber and Faber.
Sinclair, A. (1962) *Prohibition: The Era of Excesses*. London: Faber and Faber. (History of Prohibition in America.)
Wilson, G. B. (1940) *Alcohol and the Nation*. London: Nicholson and Watson. (Astonishing source book for data 1800–1935. Also provides useful bibliography of Temperance literature.)

(9 Literary descriptions

Berryman, J. (1973) *Recovery*. London: Faber and Faber.
London, J. (1914) *John Barleycorn*. London: Jonathan Cape.

Lowry, M. (1967) *Under the Volcano*. London: Jonathan Cape.
Moore, B. (1965) *The Lonely Passion of Judith Hearne*. London: Panther.
Simenon, G. (1974) *The Magician*, trans. by H. Sebba. London: Hamish Hamilton.
Westheimer, D. (1963) *The Days of Wine and Roses*. London: Corgi.

Index

Figures in italics indicate tables

gambling, 78
gastritis, 80
genetic factors in drinking, 107-8
gout, 84
group therapy, 123, 126

hallucinosis, alcoholic, 77
hangover, 27
head injuries, 83, 113
Health Education Council, 19-20, 136
heart disease, 84
Home Office Committee on the drunkenness Offender, 138
homeless alcoholic, the
  excluded from treatment, 131
  petty criminal offences, 63
  provision of services for, 14-15, 21
hostels for alcoholics, 15
hypoglycaemia, 85
hypomania, 114

impotence, 77
industry
  alcoholic beverage industry, 137, 142
  cost of alcoholism in industry, 4, 73
  employment problems, 62-3
  preventive measures in industry, 143
  use of industrial alcohol, 28
in-patient treatment of alcoholism
  admission figures as index of alcohol abuse, 4
  admission policy, 126
  alterations in practice, 13
  NHS psychiatric hospital admissions, 129, 131, 135
  medical admissions, 3, 85, 131
  selection of cases, 130-1
International Council on Alcoholism and Addictions, 143

jealousy, morbid, 78

kidney disease, 84

Korsakoff's Psychosis, 82

learning theory of alcohol dependence, 47
Librium, 34
licensing laws, 18, 23, 97-9
  effect on consumption figures, 98
  Clayson Report on, 99
  recommended policy, 139
life expectancy of alcoholics, 3
limit of safe intake of alcohol, 52, 79, 85-6, 140
liqueurs, alcohol content of, 29
liver damage, 79-80

malnutrition, 78
marital problems, 58, 60-2
marital therapy, 124
mass media, impact on public education, 20
Medical Council on Alcoholism, 16, 20
medical model of understanding alcoholism
  compared with other models, 22
  society's view of, 1-2, 21, 55, 90
  validity of concept, 54-5
  view of AA, 14
Medical Research Council, 20 148
memory, effect of alcohol on, 33
mental illness, 22, 112-14
mental subnormality, 114
methyl alcohol, toxic effects of, 85
Ministry of Health
  institutes specialized units, 13
  research spending of, 20
models of understanding drinking, 21-2, 53-6
mood
  disturbances during alcohol withdrawal, 43-4
  effect of alcohol on, 33-4
mortality rate in drinkers, 85-6, 91
  see also cirrhosis mortality rate
murder, 61, 65
muscle wasting disease, 84

smoking, 39, 78
social work counselling, 15, 62
society
  reaction to alcoholism, 1–2
  role obligations in society, 59
  social disabilities *see* disabilities, alcohol-related
special units for treatment of alcoholism, 13, 130–31
specialism in alcoholism treatment, 127, 146–47
spirits, alcohol content of, 29
stress, 104–5
success rates in treatment, 25, 129–30
suicide attempts, 75
  drinking as 'chronic suicide', 111
  in wives of alcoholics, 60
Summer Schools on Alcoholism, 16

taxation of alcohol, 18, 137
teetotalism, 85
television, role in education, 19
tension relief drinking, 109
tranquillizers, 74, 78
treatment of alcoholism
  behaviour therapy, 124
  case assessment, 121
  counselling goals, 122
  deterrent drugs, 125
  detoxification, 125–26
  intensity of care approach, 126–27
  psychotherapies, 123–24
  selection of cases for treatment, 130–32
  society's expectations of treatment, 133
  treatability of drink problems, 24–5
  treatment results, 129–30
treatment goals, 121–22, 127–28
treatment services
  planning services, 6, 21, 127
  recommended policy, 146
tuberculosis, 84

ulcers, peptic, 80
unemployment, 62

Valium 34
vitamin deficiency diseases, 82, 84

Warlingham Park Hospital, 13, 62
welfare services
  cost of, 4
  for homeless alcoholics, 14–15
West London Mission, 15
wife-battering, 4, 60
wines, alcohol content of, 29
withdrawal symptoms
  clinical description, 43–4
  causing return to drinking, 42, 44
  treatment of withdrawal, 125–26
wives of alcoholics, 4, 60–2
women
  drinking wives, 61
  drink problems in women, 4, 83
  social disapproval of women drinking, 102
World Health Organization, 7, 12, 143
  WHO definition of alcoholism, 7